BIRDS
BRITANNIA

BIRDS
BRITANNIA

STEPHEN MOSS

HOW THE BRITISH
FELL IN LOVE WITH BIRDS

Collins

FOR TONY SOPER & BILL ODDIE

Birders and broadcasters
par excellence

HarperCollins Publishers
77-85 Fulham Palace Road
London W6 8JB

www.harpercollins.co.uk

Collins is a registered trademark of HarperCollins Publishers Ltd.
First published in 2011

Text © Stephen Moss 2011

16 15 14 13 12 11
10 9 8 7 6 5 4 3 2 1

A catalogue record for this book is available from the British Library.

ISBN 978 0 00 741344 7

Collins uses papers that are natural, renewable and recyclable products made
from wood grown in sustainable forests. The manufacturing processes
conform to the environmental regulations of the country of origin.

All reasonable efforts have been made by the author to trace the copyright
owners of the material quoted in this book. In the event that the author or
publishers are notified of any mistakes or omissions by copyright owners
after publication of this book, the author and the publisher will endeavour
to rectify the position accordingly for any subsequent printing.

Printed and bound in Great Britain by Clays Ltd, St Ives plc

Mixed Sources
Product group from well-managed
forests and other controlled sources
www.fsc.org Cert no. SW-COC-001806
© 1996 Forest Stewardship Council

FSC is a non-profit international organisation established to promote
the responsible management of the world's forests. Products carrying the
FSC label are independently certified to assure consumers that they come
from forests that are managed to meet the social, economic and
ecological needs of present and future generations.

Find out more about HarperCollins and the environment at
www.harpercollins.co.uk/green

CONTENTS

INTRODUCTION

W e British are more obsessed with birds than any other nation on earth. From feeding ducks in the park to listening for the first cuckoo of spring, from inspiring some of our best-loved poetry to filling our stomachs, and from boosting the economy to providing comfort during times of crisis, birds have long been at the centre of our nation's history. This unique relationship between the British and our birds reveals as much about us as it does about the birds themselves.

As birder, author and cultural historian Mark Cocker points out: 'Bird song, bird flight, birds' residence around us, cements our relationship with them, and there is no equal in our landscape – and that's why birds are so important to the British.'

Partly, as we shall see in the opening chapter, *Garden Birds*, our passion for birds is a result of the major social changes that took place during the eighteenth and nineteenth centuries, when our ancestors moved lock, stock and barrel from a rural, agrarian existence to an urban, industrial one.

Having shifted so dramatically from the countryside to the city, in just two or three generations, they developed a powerful nostalgia for the landscapes they had left behind, and for the wild creatures that lived there, especially the birds. In response, perhaps, to their sense of loss, they decided to create their own little piece of the countryside in their new home: and the British love of gardens began to blossom. With it came a new kind of relationship with the birds that visited our gardens; a relationship that today is still one of the closest and most meaningful of all our encounters with birds.

Jumping ahead to the final chapter, *Countryside Birds*, the strength of the British love of our countryside and the birds that live there is explored in greater depth. We discover how the birds of our countryside are inextricably linked with our appreciation of the landscape and what it means to us; how we celebrated their importance to us in many different ways; and how, as they have declined, this has threatened the very nature of what we mean by 'countryside'.

But our relationship with birds has its darker side, too. The middle two chapters, on Waterbirds and Seabirds, reveal a more primal connection, expressed initially through the very basic need to hunt and kill birds for food and other commodities. Later this developed into the wider exploitation of bird populations for profit: whether for fashion or fertiliser, feathers or simply fun, the British have always been adept at making money out of birds. On a more positive side, the wholesale slaughter of these birds eventually prompted a reaction against such wanton cruelty, leading to the rise of the bird protection movement, in which the British led the world, and – along with our neighbours across the Atlantic in North America – continue to do so today.

The eighteenth and nineteenth centuries saw the development of a recreational interest in birds: largely taking the form
of shooting and killing them for sport. But during the course of
the twentieth century, and into the new millennium, our passion
for birds took a more benevolent, and less destructive, direction.
This was through the hobby, pastime or obsession (call it what
you will) of birdwatching – or birding, as it is now more usually
known. Again, Britain leads the world: with more than one million members of the RSPB, half a million people taking part in
Citizen Science projects such as the Big Garden Birdwatch, and
tens of thousands of enthusiasts actively going out to watch
birds every weekend. Along with sport, cookery and gardening,
birding has now become one of our major leisure activities, and
in a world where our concern for the environment is growing, its
popularity looks set to continue.

The impulses behind why we watch birds are almost as varied
as the people who do it – few other pastimes cross quite so many
social and demographic boundaries, appealing to people of all ages,
backgrounds and classes. As the great ornithologist and media
man James Fisher wrote at the start of the Second World War:

Among those I know of [who watch birds] are a
Prime Minister, a President, three Secretaries of
State, a charwoman, two policemen, two Kings,
two Royal Dukes, one Prince, one Princess, a
Communist, seven Labour, one Liberal, and six
Conservative Members of Parliament, several
farm-labourers earning ninety shillings a week,

a rich man who earns two or three times that
amount in every hour of the day, at least
forty-six schoolmasters, an engine-driver,
a postman, and an upholsterer.

A similar list compiled today would be even more wide-ranging and inclusive.

As to why we enjoy watching birds so much, perhaps it is because it appeals to many different human impulses and instincts, as Fisher rightly pointed out: 'The observation of birds may be a superstition, a tradition, an art, a science, a pleasure, a hobby, or a bore; this depends entirely on the nature of the observer.' *Birds Britannia* explores this eclectic passion, taking us on a journey from exploitation, through appreciation, to delight.

STEPHEN MOSS
Mark, Somerset
January 2011

GARDEN
BIRDS

O f all Britain's birds, one particular group has risen to the very top of our affections – those that have chosen to live alongside us, in our gardens. These have become the most familiar, the most loved and, in some cases, the most hated of our birds. In some ways they define our relationship with Britain's birdlife, as birder and broadcaster Bill Oddie points out: 'For many people there is nothing but garden birds – the only birds they actually see are in their garden!'

It's hardly surprising we are so obsessed with garden birds, for they perform a daily soap opera outside our back window; a soap opera whose characters reflect our own attitudes, prejudices and emotions.

These are our most familiar birds: those we see every day and interact with most in our lives. Not surprisingly, this has engendered a very deep and intimate relationship between us and the natural world, as David Attenborough reflects:

GARDEN BIRDS

No matter how small your garden is,
there will be a bird that comes to it. And they
bring a breath of the natural world, the non-
human world, and they're the one thing that
does. They're also magical, in that they suddenly
take off and disappear and you've no idea where
they've gone – yet they come back again.

And yet our relationship with garden birds is a surprisingly modern one. It is the result of some of the most dramatic changes in British society in the last hundred and fifty years.

*   *   *

We are a nation of gardeners who have become a nation of garden-bird lovers. Our long and cherished relationship with our gardens is clear from the huge popularity of television and radio programmes such as *Gardeners' World* and *Gardeners' Question Time*, as well as the plethora of gardening magazines on sale in our newsagents. This has undoubtedly helped to influence and define our relationship with the birds that live alongside us.

Today, two out of three of us feed wild birds in our gardens, spending over £150 million pounds a year in the process. This relationship brings a mutual benefit, whereby the birds are fed, and we are entertained by watching them. And for many people, this simple act of kindness to our fellow creatures is the entry point into a deeper relationship with wildlife as a whole; a relationship that may span their entire lifetime.

Yet only a century ago, most of us did not even have gardens. We took little interest in the welfare of our feathered neighbours, and were more likely to eat a Blackbird than to feed it. The very concept of 'garden birds' was meaningless – as environmental historian Rob Lambert points out, the term hadn't even been invented: '"Garden birds" is a cultural construct – these are simply birds that have taken advantage of the new suburban landscapes we have created. These are birds of the woodland edge that have moved into what we have defined as "gardens".'

As the landscape of Britain changed, so birds that had evolved to live in our woods and forests – tits, thrushes, woodpeckers and many more – found sanctuary in our gardens. They were joined by birds of more open countryside – finches, pigeons and doves – that also exploited the plentiful opportunities for food, shelter and nesting places in our backyards.

As the wider countryside became less and less suitable for birds, due to the intensification of agriculture and the resulting loss of habitat, so gardens became the prime habitat for many of these species – effectively turning them from woodland and farmland birds into what we now call 'garden birds'.

So in little more than a century, an extraordinary transformation has taken place in our relationship with the birds that live alongside us. This domestic drama runs parallel to the history and development of that very British phenomenon, the modern suburban garden. But it's a story that begins ten thousand years ago, when one adaptable little bird sought out our company for the very first time: the House Sparrow.

*　　*　　*

The House Sparrow is often taken for granted, but it is a particular favourite of birder and broadcaster Tony Soper: 'It's a small, chunky little bird, with wonderful chestnuts and browns – in a drab sort of way it's a very colourful bird. But mostly what's good about the sparrow is its behaviour – the cheeky "cockney spadger"!'

House Sparrows have lived alongside humans longer than any other wild bird – since our prehistoric ancestors first abandoned their hunter-gatherer lifestyle in favour of farming, leading to a more settled way of life, as Mark Cocker explains:

The sparrow's engagement with us is peculiarly intimate, and is rooted in the development of agriculture. Agriculture is thought to have originated in the Fertile Crescent of the Middle East, and House Sparrows probably spread across Europe, as agriculture was spread from community to community. And as they moved, they found a way to live beside us.

Sparrows found nest sites on our homes and food in our fields and farmyards. Indeed they are now only found in and around human settlements, and have spread, via deliberate and accidental introductions, across much of the globe. Today the familiar chirp of the House Sparrow can be heard in towns and cities in North and South America, Africa, Australia and New Zealand; and in many of these places they have exploited vacant ecological niches to the detriment of native species.

But in the view of Denis Summers-Smith, an amateur ornithologist who has studied sparrows for more than sixty years, their very dependence on us meant that we viewed them with suspicion from the outset: 'Sparrows, from very early on, were regarded as pests, because they fed on the cereal crops the farmers were growing.'

By the reign of Queen Elizabeth I, in the second half of the sixteenth century, sparrows had a price put on their heads, thanks to the passing of an Act of Parliament branding them as agricultural pests. As a result, people would take the head of each sparrow to the parish church where they'd be paid a small bounty.

Since that time, farming communities all over Britain have waged war on sparrows to safeguard their crops. Mark Cocker believes that this has had long-term consequences, helping to define our current relationship with this familiar little bird: 'One of the interesting things about sparrows is that they've never really lost a shyness, a difficulty of approach, in the way that Blue Tits and Robins have lost their fear of us… And I think that's to do with the way that because they ate grain they were harvested and eaten.'

But it's not all that easy to catch such a clever bird – so in the seventeenth century our ancestors turned to the Netherlands for a practical solution, according to Denis Summers-Smith:

Dutch engineers who had come over to drain the Fens brought with them what were known as 'sparrow-pots'. These were put up on farm buildings, primarily to prevent the sparrows nesting in the thatch; but also, because they were on a hook, they could be lifted off. The housewife could put her hand in the back and remove either the sparrows or the eggs, and these would very often go into a pot in the kitchen.

The number of tiny eggs required to make a decent omelette, or birds to make a pie, might appear hardly worth the trouble of collecting or catching them. Yet it must have been worthwhile, as this practice continued far longer than we might imagine – sparrows were caught and eaten in the countryside until the middle of the twentieth century.

But some Britons had already begun to take a very different view of this little bird, as a result of the biggest social change in British history. This was the wholesale migration of millions of people from the countryside into the towns, to meet the increased need for labour in factories required by the Industrial Revolution. Rural historian Jeremy Burchardt regards this as a key turning-point in the history of our nation:

In the nineteenth century the balance of population between rural England and urban England changed quite dramatically. In the early nineteenth century the great majority of people lived in the countryside; by 1900 only about one in five people did. So we had effectively changed from being a rural nation into being an urban nation in the space of a few generations.

Given how dependent House Sparrows were on humans, it's not surprising that, as we moved into towns, they were the one bird that came along with us. They were partly able to do so because, as historian Jenny Uglow explains, the differences between urban and rural areas were not all that great:

> One aspect to the growing cities is that
> they were still terribly close to the country; not
> just physically, but the fact that there were a lot
> of agricultural animals actually in the city. You
> had horses everywhere, you had stables, and also
> in the parks – like in St James's Park in London
> – there were cows, there were sheep.
> So those birds which thrive on dung and seeds
> like the sparrow could find the city
> quite a happy home.

Arguably sparrows enjoyed better living conditions in Victorian cities than did much of the human population. Denis Summers-Smith notes that these newly built dwellings created to house the growing human population provided safe for the birds too: places to nest, where they were safe from attack by birds of prey and cats.

But the other reason for the success of sparrows in our towns and cities was a change in our attitude towards them. People rather welcomed the presence of this little bird, which perhaps reminded them of their ancestral home.

The townsfolk's new-found affection for sparrows was undoubtedly a reaction to urbanisation – a disorientating process that cut millions of Britons off from wild nature, and at the same time made them nostalgic for their rural past. This was the start of a very new way of looking at the 'countryside' – not as a place where people lived and worked, but as a rural idyll of peace and harmony. This view would later come to define the relationship between town and country – a relationship that persists even today.

Meanwhile, back in the ever-growing cities of the Victorian era, the working classes and the urban poor found themselves living in densely packed housing with little if any outdoor space, and no trees or greenery. But they found one way to reconnect with the birds of the countryside – not outside the home, but within it.

*   *   *

Like us, the Victorians were obsessed with birds. Unlike us, they preferred to keep them in cages, rather than watch them in the wild. The cagebird craze became a big part of domestic life, and as well as what historian of science Helen Macdonald calls 'the usual suspects' – Canaries and Budgerigars – the Victorians also kept a very wide range of British species, including Wheatears and thrushes, as well as more typical cagebirds such as finches.

These birds were trapped in vast numbers – tens of thousands were caught at popular sites such as the South Downs in Sussex – and sold in London markets such as Club Row in London's East End. They were caught using a variety of ingenious methods: smearing branches and twigs of trees with 'bird-lime' (a glutinous substance made from, amongst other things, holly bark), and by using large nets, which were laid out onto the ground and triggered by pulling a piece of string. Decoy birds were often tethered next to the nets, as a way of luring wild birds in. Spring and autumn were the main bird-catching seasons, as they coincided with the seasonal migrations of the birds.

The Victorian journalist and social reformer Henry Mayhew, who in 1851 wrote *London Labour and the London Poor*, made a special study of the bird-catchers. He reported that the majority of birds caught were Linnets, an attractive little finch with a sweet and melodious song. Up to 70,000 Linnets a year were being trapped, and sold for three or four pence each – though mature birds with particularly good songs could be sold for as much as half-a-crown (about £12 at today's values). Goldfinches were also popular, and sold for between sixpence and one shilling a head – equivalent to a few pounds today. For the people involved in bird-catching, it must have been a profitable trade.

The Linnet's widespread popularity as a cagebird was celebrated in the lyrics of the popular music-hall hit, 'My Old Man', written by Charles Collins and Fred Leigh:

My old man said 'follow the van,
And don't dilly dally on the way!'
Off went the van with my old man in it,
I walked behind with me old cock linnet...

A more literary example can be found in Charles Dickens's novel *Bleak House*, in which one memorable scene, also shown in the BBC television adaptation in 2005, dramatises the Victorian passion for cagebirds. One character, old Miss Flite, is embroiled in a long-running court case, but takes comfort in her collection of birds in cages, which she vows to release once the case is finally settled.

Cagebirds weren't kept for purely aesthetic reasons, but because they brought a reminder of the Victorian city-dwellers' rural past into their homes, according to Jenny Uglow: 'The song of the bird was like the music of the country; and you could close your eyes, and listen to the bird sing, and be transported back to the countryside that you came from. For people in the city, the wild bird becomes an emblem of the freedom they have lost.'

To our modern sensibilities, the notion that birds in cages could be symbols of freedom may seem bizarre. And indeed for some time there had been growing numbers of people objecting to the practice, including the poet and reformer William Blake. In 'Auguries of Innocence', written in the early nineteenth century but not published until 1863, he unequivocally condemns bird-keeping, in a celebrated couplet:

A robin redbreast in a cage
Puts all heaven in a rage.

According to the historian Keith Thomas, author of *Man and the Natural World*, wild birds were often invoked as symbols of an Englishman's freedom, while a growing movement objected to the cruelty involved – not simply imprisoning the birds, but also blinding them, a common practice supposed to improve the quality of their song. But the trade continued, and as Jenny Uglow points out, for many Victorians keeping birds in cages was not regarded as cruel in any way. She cites contemporary accounts of species such as Goldfinches being happy in their cage, and appearing to sing more frequently than they did in the wild.

Not surprisingly, the most popular cagebirds were those with the most attractive song, including the Nightingale, justly famed as the greatest and most varied of all our native songsters. But this insectivorous bird would have been very tricky to keep and look after as a cagebird, as Tim Birkhead, author of *The Wisdom of Birds*, explains: 'The Nightingale was a very difficult bird to keep in captivity, requiring live food such as worms and insects, and as a result having very wet droppings, so you had to go to a lot of trouble to keep it – both to feed it and to keep it clean.'

Fed up with the problems of keeping such a fussy bird, the Victorians looked around for a more convenient alternative. They found it not in a wild British bird, but in an imported exotic species, the Canary which, as Tim Birkhead puts it, 'knocked the Nightingale off its perch'.

*   *   *

But whether exotic or British, caged birds served another purpose beyond their song and attractive appearance. Birds in cages were regarded by the Victorians as excellent examples of moral instruction, especially as a way of teaching children, as Tim Birkhead explains: 'If you had a pair of Canaries in a cage, and they were breeding, you could see "mum and dad" feeding the chicks – they were, in a way, like a model human couple.'

Because the Victorians believed birds paired for life, unlike many other creatures, the Christian Church had singled them out for special attention. One clergyman was particularly influential in shaping attitudes to birds at this time. Tony Soper notes: 'The Reverend Francis Orpen Morris was typical of the clergy of his day, in that he regarded all bird life as moral creatures from which we had to learn.'

F. O. Morris, as he is generally known, was one of the great Victorian popularisers of birds. In his long life – he lived more than eighty years – he published numerous books on many and varied subjects, including British birds. His most celebrated work, *A History of British Birds*, appeared from 1851 to 1857.

Like many Victorian works, both of fiction and non-fiction, *A History of British Birds* was published in regular 'partworks' costing a shilling each, which made it accessible to a very wide audience. Eventually bound into six hefty volumes, it was subsequently reprinted at regular intervals, and even today hand-coloured plates from this work can be found in antique shops all over the country.

Popular, the Reverend Morris's work may certainly have been; accurate and informative it was not. This damning verdict, written in 1917 by ornithological bibliographers Mullens and Swann, is fairly typical:

Of this it may be said that, although one of the most voluminous and popular works on the subject, and financially most successful (thousands of pounds having been made out of successive editions), yet it has never occupied any very important position among the histories of British birds. Morris was too voluminous to be accurate, and too didactic to be scientific. He

accepted records and statements without discrimination, and consequently his work abounds with errors and mistakes.

Their verdict isn't entirely negative, and acknowledges that popularity has its virtues: 'Yet as a book for amateur ornithologists it has charmed and delighted for more than half a century, and it had for many years the great merit of being almost the only work at a moderate price to give a fairly accurate and coloured figure of every species.'

But like so many Victorian clergymen who used nature as a way of teaching morals to their flock, Morris's lack of a basic understanding of biology let him down – in his case, very badly indeed. For amongst his favourite birds – and one he frequently invoked as an example to his parishioners and readers – was the Hedge Sparrow, now known as the Dunnock.

Despite its superficial resemblance to the House Sparrow, the Dunnock is in fact completely unrelated to that species. It is the only common and widespread representative in Britain of a small family known as the accentors: mostly birds of high mountains and rocky slopes, found entirely in the temperate regions of Europe and Asia. Its name, dating back to the fifteenth century, simply means 'little brown bird'.

Dunnocks are rather retiring birds, easy to overlook, as Tony Soper notes: 'The Dunnock is a shy little bird, a reclusive little bird, that walks around the bottom of the bird table picking up the crumbs. And yet it's one of these birds that, when you get a really good, close-up look at it, has a really fine plumage, with pinkish legs and a nice little thin bill.'

GARDEN BIRDS

It was this shyness and modesty that appealed so strongly to the Reverend Morris, as Tim Birkhead points out: 'Humble in its behaviour, drab and sober in its dress, this was the perfect model for how all his parishioners should behave.'

But then again, the Reverend Morris didn't know the truth about the Dunnock. As Jeremy Mynott, author of *Birdscapes*, notes, the sex life of this species is truly extraordinary: 'It enters into every relationship possible: polygamy, polygyny, polyandry, promiscuity… you name it, the Dunnock does it!'

Sometime during the early part of the year, just as the days begin to lengthen, male Dunnocks leave their hiding places in the shrubbery and are miraculously transformed from shy wallflowers into loud, self-confident show-offs.

Usually sitting in full view on a hedge, tree or fence post, the male sings his rather flat, tuneless song from dawn to dusk. Like any other songbird at this time of the year, he's trying to attract a mate. Unlike many other birds, he won't be content with just one.

Having formed a pair-bond with a female, the male Dunnock spends much of the day following her doggedly around – demonstrating the apparently faithful behaviour that so appealed to Morris. But he's not doing this out of devotion, but jealousy; because every female Dunnock is keeping half an eye out for a neighbouring male – a rival to her mate. If she can shake off his attentions for a moment or two she will mate with the other male, as Tim Birkhead explains: 'Dunnocks, instead of breeding as a conventional pair, often breed as a trio: two males paired simultaneously with one female. The female wants both males to mate with her, because if both males mate with her they will both help to rear her chicks.'

Despite her mate's obsessive guarding, we know that the female Dunnock does often manage to mate with another male. Clutches of Dunnock's eggs from the same nest have been examined, revealing that the chicks may have several different fathers. The male isn't always the victim – even while he is devotedly feeding his first brood, he may well sneak off and feed another set of chicks in a nest nearby.

It is thought that this extraordinarily complex breeding strategy evolved because there are normally far fewer female Dunnocks than male ones, which allows them to have the upper hand.

This scandalous behaviour was only revealed in the 1990s, by a group of scientists in Cambridge, led by Professor Nick Davies. It was first shown to a wider public in 1998, in the BBC series *The Life of Birds*, presented by David Attenborough. Viewers were astonished to see the means by which the first male tries to make sure that his sperm fertilises the female, so that the chicks will be his. As Tim Birkhead points out, his first line of defence is to copulate at an incredible rate – up to one hundred times in a single day. But the male Dunnock has another trick up his sleeve.

Using slow-motion film cameras and a lot of time, skill and patience, wildlife cameraman Barrie Britton eventually managed to capture the split-second moment at which the male – knowing that the female has already mated with his rival – pecks persistently at her cloaca until she expels a packet of sperm from the other male. Only then does the first male actually 'do the business'. It's a case of 'blink and you'll miss it', as Tim Birkhead explains: 'As the droplet of sperm comes out he looks at it, and then copulates with her. The other thing that's absolutely remarkable is that those copulations in the Dunnock are so fast – it's about a tenth of a second, which must be almost the fastest bird copulation there is. He basically just flies over her…'

So in choosing the Dunnock as such a fine example of morality and fidelity, the Reverend Francis Orpen Morris could hardly have got it more wrong. As Tony Soper remarks: 'I'm afraid that the only moral you can draw from them is "every man for himself!"'

Presumably if the Reverend Morris knew what we know today about the Dunnock, he would be turning in his grave.

*　　*　　*

Morality was not the only aspect of Victorian culture shaping our fledgling relationship with the birdlife in our towns and gardens. The rapidly growing humane movement also played an important role, by campaigning for compassionate treatment of all God's creatures. At the centre of this urban mass movement were children's humane societies, such as the RSPCA's Band of Mercy, and the Dicky Bird Society, founded in 1876 by W. E. Adams.

William Edwin Adams was a truly extraordinary man. His life story is a classic Victorian tale of endeavour, persistence and sacrifice in the service of others. Born in 1832, in Cheltenham, to poor, working-class parents, Adams became one of the leading social reformers of his day. After leaving school at fourteen, Adams began work as a journeyman printer, and then became a journalist, writing mainly on the burning social issues of his day, and getting involved in the new political movement of socialism.

In 1862, at the age of thirty, Adams had a stroke of luck. Asked to contribute a column to the *Newcastle Weekly Chronicle*, two years later he became its editor, a post he held for more than a third of a century, until he retired in 1900.

By then, Adams had become heavily involved in the movement to educate children in a more humane way, and so he began a newspaper column under the pseudonym 'Uncle Toby', dispensing advice to young readers. In 1876, he founded the Dicky Bird Society, aimed at encouraging humane behaviour towards animals in children.

A key aspect of this behaviour was feeding wild birds, and this was included in the pledge taken by new members of the Dicky Bird Society: 'I hereby promise to be kind to all living things, to protect them to the utmost of my power, to feed the birds in the winter-time, and never to take or destroy a nest.'

Today we take feeding birds for granted, but in Victorian times it was quite unusual, even in towns and cities. By encouraging children to feed wild birds, the Dicky Bird Society, and others like it, promoted a pastime that would go on to forge a lasting bond between the British people and what would eventually become our 'garden birds'.

The Dicky Bird Society was a highly successful organisation, which continued to run until 1940, attracting hundreds of thousands of children throughout the country, and gaining public support from such Victorian luminaries as John Ruskin, Alfred Lord Tennyson and Florence Nightingale. Together with other children's humane organisations they could boast millions of members, some of whom came from surprising places, according to social historian Frederick Milton, who has made a special study of the society: 'There is a letter written to the Dicky Bird Society from children in Dover workhouse, which tells Uncle Toby that they were collecting crumbs from their table to feed to the birds the next day.'

As Frederick Milton notes, this eagerness to engage with feeding birds was not confined to children living in poverty: 'As the nineteenth century progressed, the number of people actually feeding the birds visibly increased. There was a brand-new generation of individuals who were far more interested in garden birds and their welfare.'

But not everyone in Victorian society thought it necessary, or indeed desirable, to feed birds, as Rob Lambert explains:

The Victorians were caught up in a massive ethical dilemma about feeding garden birds. On the one hand, Victorian values and society were dominated by the concept of 'Self-Help' [the title of a book and movement led by Samuel Smiles] – you had to look after yourself, and couldn't depend on the state for welfare and support in hard times. And they extended this moral code onto the birdlife, so therefore the Victorians believed that by feeding the garden birds, you somehow made them indolent, lazy, and dependent on welfare.

These attitudes would be changed by a series of very hard winters, which pushed birds to the edge of starvation. In particular the winter of 1890–1 saw long spells of ice and snow, and national newspapers began to urge their readers to feed the birds. In the centre of London, the nature writer W. H. Hudson witnessed working men giving scraps from their meagre supplies of food. As Rob Lambert points out, this coincided with a shift in attitudes in the country as a whole:

> Victorian Britain was also dominated
> by these emerging new sensibilities; by this
> wave of humanitarianism that developed decade
> by decade, which was extremely powerful. And
> the Victorians couldn't bear to see suffering, so
> when hard winters kicked in, and birds began to
> die in Victorian gardens, there was then a battle
> for control over the Victorian mind – and in the
> end it was the humanitarianism that won, and
> the Victorians fed their garden birds
> in times of great peril.

A major winner from this change in attitudes towards feeding birds was the Robin. This had already become firmly established as the nation's favourite bird, according to cultural historian Christopher Frayling:

> There's a very rich folklore for the
> Robin that goes way back – for example where
> did the Robin gets its red breast? It got its red
> breast because it plucked a thorn from the crown
> of thorns – as Jesus was on his way to Gethsemane,

a drop of Jesus's blood falls onto the bird, and thereafter the Robin has a red breast. So it's associated in a very deep way with the New Testament. So Robins, by Shakespeare's time, and possibly long before that, are associated with charity and piety.

Historian Keith Thomas notes that the Robin was accorded almost supernatural powers, as in this seventeenth-century poem penned by Margaret Cavendish, Marchioness of Newcastle:

Man superstitiously dares not hurt me,
For if I'm killed or hurt, ill luck shall be.

Robins were also associated with death: if one tapped on a window or came into a house, it was thought that one of the occupants would soon die. Given that Robins would frequently appear on the doorstep in search of food, especially during harsh winter weather, this belief may seem rather odd – but perhaps it marks the unseen boundary between regarding this endearing little bird as a 'wild pet', and not allowing it to cross over the boundary into our domestic lives.

Whatever the ambiguities of our relationship with the Robin, by the Victorian era its position in our popular culture had become even more deeply entrenched. Jeremy Mynott tells the complex story behind our present-day association of Robins with Christmas, which arose in the middle of the nineteenth century:

Robins appear on Christmas cards through a
rather strange process of causation. Robins gave
their name to the first postmen, who wore red
tunics, and were therefore called 'robins'. And on
some of the early Christmas cards delivered by
these postmen, the Robin was often pictured with
a postcard in its mouth, delivering the letter
like a postman. So the Robin gave its name
to the postman, and the postman gave
his role to the Robin.

Another obvious reason for the connection of Robins with the
festive season is that they often come into gardens in search of
food, especially during spells of ice and snow. But whatever the
reason, every year since, highly sentimental images of Robins
have appeared on our Christmas cards, an annual renewal of our
commitment to them.

*　　*　　*

By the start of the twentieth century the foundations of today's
special relationship with the birds living alongside us had already
been laid. Although we didn't yet call them 'garden birds', a
growing number of people regarded these wild creatures with a
sentimentality that would have been inconceivable to their rural
ancestors. But this developing picture of harmony was about to
be severely tested, with the coming of the First World War.

GARDEN BIRDS

In August 1914, within days of the outbreak of the conflict, the Defence of the Realm Act was passed. This draconian piece of legislation outlawed many activities, and amendments to the Act later included the wastage of food. Almost overnight, feeding garden birds became illegal, and people were even prosecuted for doing so, including an elderly woman living in Surrey, Sophia Stuart.

According to a report in the *Daily Mail*, she appeared at Woking Crown Court, charged with the offence of giving bread to wild birds. In her defence, the poor woman stated that she had lost her only son, who had been killed fighting in Mesopotamia; that all she used were the dirty bottom crusts she could not eat. Moreover, she maintained that she had fed the birds for seventy years – and would continue to do so, whatever the court decided.

For this small act of defiance, she was fined two guineas – the equivalent of several hundred pounds today. For Britain's garden birds, as well as its people, the world had certainly changed for the worse.

The war also cut off supplies of nestboxes, which had been imported from Germany by the RSPB and had proved very popular with householders. The inventor of the nestbox, Baron Hans von Berlepsch, had even been granted the position of 'Honorary Fellow' by the RSPB, in recognition of what he had done to help conserve Britain's birds. The coming of war between Britain and Germany put paid to this fine example of Anglo-German co-operation, and as a result our birds had to revert to finding natural nest sites.

One familiar species wasn't simply deprived of food and nesting sites, but became one of the first casualties of war on the Home Front. House Sparrows had long been persecuted in the countryside because they ate grain, thereby depriving farmers of part of their harvest. But now people in cities, towns and suburbs also became concerned about the threat they posed to the nation's food supply, so they joined 'sparrow clubs'. These organisations may sound benevolent, but they had a very sinister aim, according to Mark Cocker:

The sparrow club was a way of dealing with this urban and suburban 'vermin species'. It involved a cluster of working-class people who would bring in their tallies from the sparrows they had killed in their allotment or their garden, and the person who had killed the greatest number of sparrows would win a silver cup for that year.

One poster, issued by the grandly named Bedfordshire War Agricultural Executive Committee, reveals the rewards available for those who were prepared to catch and kill sparrows, just as their ancestors had done in Elizabethan times. Bounties offered by the local parish council were a penny for a dozen sparrows' eggs, tuppence for a dozen unfledged sparrows, and threepence for a dozen fledged ones – which meant that a skilled collector could amass a tidy sum given that, at the time, a pint of beer would have cost about sixpence. Rats provided an even higher reward: as much as two shillings per dozen, though they were presumably harder to catch.

The methods used to catch the sparrows themselves varied considerably, from large nets to specially made cane traps advertised in catalogues. These inevitably caught all sorts of other small birds in the process, as those doing the catching weren't always either very expert or discriminating. And once caught, the birds weren't all immediately killed, as Frederick Milton explains: 'They were taken to gentleman's clubs or to pubs, where they were then used as targets for trap-shooting.'

Ironically, the actions of the sparrow clubs may have themselves contributed to food shortages, as they did not take into account the beneficial effects sparrows had on killing harmful pests such as insects, especially during the spring when the adult birds were feeding their young.

And ultimately, even though hundreds of thousands of sparrows were killed by sparrow clubs during the war, it may all have been in vain. Because the culls took place in late summer – at the end of the breeding season, when numbers were at their peak – the killing appears to have had very little impact on the overall population.

Ironically, it was what we did in peacetime that would bring about a collapse in sparrow numbers. During the 1920s and 1930s, the coming of motor vehicles meant the end for the main form of urban transport since people had first moved into cities: the horse. The internal combustion engine – in private cars, buses and taxicabs – soon triumphed. Horse-drawn transport rapidly began to vanish from our city streets.

And with it went our old friend – and occasional enemy – the House Sparrow. City sparrows had long depended on horse feed and undigested seeds in horse droppings for food. So the replacement of horses by cars and buses deprived them of a vital resource. Sparrow expert Denis Summers-Smith believes that this marked the start of the House Sparrow's long, slow decline – a decline which, as we shall discover, continues today.

BIRDS BRITANNIA

*   *   *

Without even trying, we had reduced the numbers of the House Sparrow – the original garden bird – forever. But for many other garden birds, as for many householders, the period between the two world wars would see the dawn of a golden age – the start of what Christopher Frayling calls 'the garden bird phenomenon': 'If you read books about birds in the eighteenth, nineteenth and early twentieth centuries, no one talks about "garden birds". It goes with the growth of suburbia.'

And grow suburbia certainly did. In just two decades, from 1920 to 1939, four million new homes were built across Britain, many of them in the 'new towns' such as Letchworth, Welwyn Garden City and Stevenage, on the outskirts of London; others in the suburbs of the capital itself. Moreover, for the first time in our nation's history, the vast majority of these had proper gardens. Jenny Uglow believes that this came down to large-scale planning at a national level: 'First of all there was the planning of new suburbs, with wider roads and trees, and long gardens. It's the continuation of a passionate Victorian idea, that we must live close to nature, in order to live a good quality of life, and to be fully human.'

The interwar housing boom was the biggest garden creation scheme ever seen. Collectively, these new gardens provided a whole new man-made habitat for the birds to colonise. But it took some time for us to appreciate the wider ecological benefits this would bring – a network of 'mini-habitats' creating a much greater whole than the sum of the individual parts, as Mark Cocker notes: 'The importance of gardens in cities is classically

38

revealed if you have an aerial photograph, where you rise up above, and instead of the gardens being separate, discrete, unimportant scraps of land around each house, they form an aggregate of "semi-woodland" habitats that are actually very important, and often support a substantial diversity of birds.' Today, gardens cover more than one million acres in area – bigger than all our nature reserves put together – and provide a vital haven for many species of songbird that would otherwise be in serious trouble, because of what is happening in the wider countryside.

The creation of the modern suburban garden during the 1920s and 1930s set the stage on which the relationship between homeowners and garden birds would play out over the rest of the twentieth century. And one species would lead the way: that quintessential garden bird, the Robin.

*   *   *

No other British bird inspires quite the same affection as the Robin. Indeed the name itself is actually a nickname – just as our ancestors referred to the 'Jenny Wren' and 'Tom Tit', so the bird officially known as the 'Redbreast' acquired the prefix 'Robin Redbreast'. Gradually the second part of this was dropped, and today we use only the nickname for this familiar little bird.

Part of our great affection for the Robin stems from their confiding behaviour, as Tim Birkhead explains: 'Having a wild bird like a Robin come and alight on your hand to feed really does help to form a bond between us and them, and just makes them incredibly popular.'

And their fondness for earthworms has engendered a very special relationship with gardeners, as Mark Cocker attests: 'For anybody who is turning over soil, from the gravedigger to the lady digging her rose bed, the Robin's cupboard love will triumph, and they'll attend your operations with great care!'

We now know that long before human beings came along, Robins would carefully follow large animals, especially those that dig for food, such as wild boars, in order to grab a worm or two. In Britain, where these bigger mammals had mostly disappeared, the Robin transferred its affections to human beings; whereas on the European mainland, the Robin remains a shy, woodland bird.

But despite the Robin being a very common and familiar species in Britain, even by the 1930s most aspects of its behaviour were virtually unknown. This was all to change when, for the very first time in the long and intimate relationship between us and Robins, one man decided to delve a little deeper into the bird's behaviour.

His name was David Lack, and he would go on to become one of our leading ornithologists. He pioneered the new science of population biology, notably through his detailed studies of a fascinating group of birds found on the Galapagos Islands, known as Darwin's finches. He was also, for more than a quarter of a century, Director of the prestigious Edward Grey Institute for Field Ornithology in Oxford. But in the early 1930s, after leaving Cambridge University, he had followed a more humble calling: taking a job as a schoolmaster at Dartington College, Devon.

One of the most abundant birds in the school grounds was the Robin, and Lack decided to make a study of this common and, as was thought, familiar bird. What he discovered would change the way we regarded the Robin forever.

Lack pioneered a simple but highly effective research method that is so commonly used today it is taken for granted. So that he could identify each bird, and work out the implications of every aspect of their day-to-day behaviour, he trapped all the Robins in the area, and gave them individual colour rings.

One of his first discoveries pulled the rug from under the cherished idea that each of us has a particular Robin returning to our garden, year after year – as Lack found, most Robins live for a year or two, at most. In 1943, a decade after he began his research, Lack published his findings in a slim volume, *The Life of the Robin*. As a young birdwatcher growing up in Plymouth, just down the road from Dartington, Tony Soper recalls his amazement on first reading the book: 'I was absolutely knocked out by the realisation that the Robin we had in the garden was not the same Robin we had last week, or the week before; and certainly not the same Robin as the year before!'

The Robin's traditional reputation was further undermined by the next part of Lack's research. Many years later, in 1969, the BBC wildlife documentary *The Private Life of the Robin* revealed Lack's findings in all their colourful, gory detail to an amazed audience.

Lack had discovered that unlike most birds, which use colour primarily to attract a mate, the Robin's red breast has a very different purpose. It has been described as 'war paint' – used to drive away any rival entering the Robin's territory.

To prove that this was the case, Lack carried out a simple but highly effective experiment. He placed a dead, stuffed Robin in a prominent position in a male Robin's territory, then stood back to see what would happen. To his astonishment, the territory holder viciously attacked the stuffed bird, pecking repeatedly at its head, and pulling off whole clumps of feathers with its bill. As the commentary of *The Private Life of the Robin* put it, 'our pretty robin redbreast turns out to be a very belligerent fellow.'

Lack's book on Robin behaviour became a surprise bestseller. *The Life of the Robin* also inspired a new generation of naturalists, including David Attenborough: 'The notion that you could take one species and write a whole book in which you dealt with territory, song, behavioural postures, and so on, was a revelation – and as far as I know this was the first time that one particular bird was given that kind of intensive treatment.'

It is more than half a century since David Lack unmasked the Robin as a short-lived, feisty little bird. And yet in many ways, despite Lack's revelations, the sentimental Victorian image of it persists today, as Mark Cocker notes: 'There's this curious disconnect between our notion of the "friendly Robin" – the bird that we love, the bird of our garden, the bird on our Christmas cards – that is entwined with notions of being British. And on the other hand there's the real Robin!'

By the time *The Life of the Robin* was published, Britain had been at war again for four long years. And as garden historian Jane Fearnley-Whittingstall notes, the British garden was being completely redesigned as part of the war effort: 'As far as the garden was concerned, the Ministry of Food realised there was an enormous unused land resource right there, in people's gardens. And the top priority was to produce as much food, at home, as we possibly could.'

The Dig for Victory campaign was instigated soon after the start of the war. Run by the charismatic Minister of Food, Lord

Woolton, the campaign instructed people to convert their flower-beds into vegetable patches, so that they could produce their own food to supplement their meagre rations. This helped reduce dependence on imported food, whose supplies had swiftly dried up because of the hostilities.

Posters, pamphlets and memorable government propaganda films on cinema newsreels all helped to spread the minister's message:

> You may not be lucky enough to own an ideal kitchen garden like this, but a flowerbed will grow beetroots just as well as begonias, and there may be room for vegetables on top of the Anderson Shelter, or in your backyard, or even on that flat roof – and surely, isn't an hour in the garden better than an hour in the queue?

Home-grown fruit and vegetables may have helped to liven up monotonous wartime rations but they also proved attractive to birds. And for the second time in a generation, garden birds discovered we were fickle friends, as Jane Fearnley-Whittingstall recalls: 'The birds did of course become the gardener's enemy, in a much stronger way when your diet depended on protecting your crops from the birds. Gardeners always have had – and especially at this time – a love-hate relationship with the birds of the garden.'

So people came up with ingenious strategies to keep birds off their precious fruit and veg, including home-made nets created from wooden sticks and cotton thread. But unlike the situation in the First World War that had given rise to the sparrow clubs, this time the government recognised that birds played a vital role in killing agricultural pests, so there were no longer calls for wholesale culls.

Nevertheless, birds continued to suffer: at a time when many people were close to starving themselves, they were hardly likely to put out waste food for the birds to eat. The Ministry of Food urged people to either eat leftovers, or recycle them, so scraps once given to the birds now ended up in communal pig bins.

Birds also suffered badly during two of the hardest winters of the twentieth century, 1939–40 and 1946–7. Even though the second of these freezing winters occurred nearly two years after the end of the war, this was still a lean time for garden birds, as food rationing continued to be in force for almost a decade after the end of the conflict.

*   *   *

Britain now entered a period of austerity. This would continue right up to the end of the 1950s, when increased economic prosperity finally led Prime Minister Harold Macmillan to make his famous pronouncement that 'most of our people have never had it so good.' But curiously, our attitudes to gardens – and our attitudes to garden birds – began to change long before this, as Jenny Uglow points out: 'There was a slight reaction, and people wanted gardens to be places of colour and scent, and smell…'

Gardening for pleasure was back on the agenda, and part of the pleasure was communing with wildlife. This was reflected, in

1945, by the publication of a little book called *Garden Birds*, published in the 'King Penguin' series. *Garden Birds* was written by the secretary of the RSPB, Phyllis Barclay-Smith.

Barclay-Smith was a tough, no-nonsense woman in a largely male-dominated world. She served for more than half a century as the assistant secretary of the RSPB, where she was affectionately nicknamed 'The Dragon', and was once described (by the leading conservationist Max Nicholson) as 'the queen bee in her global hive'.

She was also one of the very first people to realise the enormous potential of winning converts to the conservation cause through the birds people saw every day from their back window. The title of her book was the very first time in Britain that the term 'garden birds' had appeared in print, and marked a turning point in the way we thought about them.

Garden Birds was, as you might expect from the author's character, relentlessly no-nonsense and practical in its approach, as Jenny Uglow notes:

She begins by saying that because of industrialisation and the growth of the town, our garden birds are threatened; and that we must make habitats for them. She tells you what trees to plant, where the birds like to nest, and so on. Welcoming the birds back, and not making the garden fiercely productive, is a wonderful reaction to the ferocity of war.

The design of post-war housing also reinforced these trends. In most Victorian and Edwardian homes the kitchen was at the side of the house, out of sight of the back garden. But post-war architects often placed the kitchen at the back of the house, with a clear view of the garden. Jenny Uglow believes this made a huge difference to the growth of interest in garden birds: 'The number of sinks I've seen which look down the garden, and you put objects of interest and entertainment out there, such as the bird table. And so you look from the sink, which is the epitome of drudgery, into the garden, which is the epitome of freedom – and there are these birds, coming and going.'

Outside, the nation's second-favourite bird – the Blue Tit – was getting up to some novel antics. This was reported by presenter Chris Trace on the children's television programme *Blue Peter*, in the early 1960s: 'It's not only humans who enjoy a drink of milk. People living all over the country are getting up in the mornings and finding their milk bottle tops torn off, and some of the milk missing...'

Actually it was the cream – not the milk – that was missing. Blue Tits and Great Tits were pecking through the foil tops of bottles left on the doorstep, to get at the rich cream which, being lighter than the milk, had floated to the top. Incredibly, the practice had first been observed in Southampton in 1921, when milk bottles had cardboard tops; but it really took off during the 1950s, when the entire British population of Blue Tits appeared to learn how to get at the cream almost overnight.

This may have looked like an example of evolution in action, but as Tim Birkhead reveals, it was actually a case of individual birds watching and learning from each other, as they always do:

Blue Tits and Great Tits are inquisitive birds, always poking around, peeling off bits of bark and lifting up leaves looking for food items, and peeling off the lid of a milk bottle is not that different really. Birds are doing these things all the time – it's just with the milk bottles we could see it happening. It was like a little window into their world.

These weren't the only culprits. According to ornithologist James Fisher, writing in 1957, at least eleven different species of bird had by then been observed opening milk bottles in Britain: Blue, Great, Coal and Marsh Tits, Blackbird, Robin, Chaffinch, Starling, Song Thrush, Dunnock, and of course our cheeky friend the House Sparrow. The practice was also observed abroad: with Great Spotted Woodpeckers in the Danish capital Copenhagen, Jackdaws elsewhere in Denmark, and the Steller's Jay in parts of western North America. Fisher, and his colleague Dr Robert Hinde, ascribed the behaviour to 'an insatiable curiosity worthy of Kipling's Elephant's Child'.

But even before the delivery of milk to the doorstep went into decline, the tits stopped pecking at the foil tops because of our changing tastes. As we became more health-conscious we switched to homogenised and skimmed milk – thus removing the cream from the top of the bottle.

According to the RSPB, the practice appears to have died out somewhere around the turn of the millennium. Because Blue Tits are so short-lived – typically surviving for just one or two years

– within a decade or so the knowledge handed down from parent to youngster no longer included the ability to raid milk bottles.

*　　*　　*

Most people didn't begrudge the tits their share of the cream, perhaps because they were amongst the earliest birds to establish themselves in suburbia. But the post-war period also saw the arrival of two newcomers to the British suburban scene – a dove and a parakeet. The very different welcomes they received would challenge our ideas of what it meant to be British.

The first newcomer, the Collared Dove, arrived almost unnoticed. This was perhaps because it doesn't have a very glamorous or exciting image, as Mark Cocker confesses: 'I love all birds, but there's something essentially very boring about the Collared Dove! Somebody I know described its song as like a rather bored football fan – "U-ni-ted… U-ni-ted…" There is something rather dreary about Collared Doves, and they are beige in colour, but they conceal an incredible story of expansion.'

Originally from India, the Collared Dove had slowly extended its range westward to reach Turkey by the sixteenth century, and the Balkans by the beginning of the twentieth century. Then, in the 1930s, the species began a steady westward surge across Europe, reaching Hungary in 1932, Germany in 1945 (where it is known as the 'television dove' because of its habit of perching on rooftop aerials!), the Netherlands in 1947, and France in 1952.

It took a little longer to make the leap across the North Sea. But then, in 1956, a pair of Collared Doves was discovered in a walled garden in north Norfolk – found, ironically, because the observer could not identify the birds' unfamiliar cooing call. As a keen young birder, Bill Oddie recalls making a special trip to East Anglia to see that very first breeding pair: 'I think one of the least glamorous twitches I ever went on was to north Norfolk, to see a pair of Collared Doves, which are ten a penny now. Somebody must have noticed them, because I think they'd been there about a year, and bred, before they were announced to the world.'

That particular pair, in a garden in the village of Overstrand, near Cromer, successfully raised two young. From then on the species never looked back. By 1960, just four years after the initial colonisation, Collared Doves had bred in Scotland, Wales and Ireland, and by 1966 had successfully bred at least once in every English county.

Within a decade it had been classed as a pest species, and today the Collared Dove breeds throughout Britain and Ireland, from Shetland in the north to the Isles of Scilly in the south – an estimated total of well over a quarter of a million breeding pairs. Collared Doves have even been found in North America, although whether they arrived there naturally or escaped from captivity is open to debate.

The success of the Collared Dove is partly due to its adaptability – the species thrives equally well in towns, suburbs and villages – and partly due to its extraordinary ability to breed in every month of the year, with up to six broods. Once they fledge, immature birds tend to travel long distances, aiding the species' rapid spread.

Despite his reservations, Mark Cocker salutes its success: 'Certainly they've adapted to urban and suburban environments in an incredibly positive way, and it must now be one of the ten most common birds in the British garden.'

It is – just. In the RSPB's Big Garden Birdwatch survey, which took place over one weekend in January 2010, the Collared Dove squeezed into ninth place, being found in just over half of all gardens surveyed; whereas in the British Trust for Ornithology's year-round Garden BirdWatch survey it came tenth, and was found in 72 per cent of gardens. There's no doubt that this invader from the east is now well and truly here to stay.

Unlike the Collared Dove there was little chance of our second newcomer – the Ring-necked, or as it is sometimes called, Rose-ringed, Parakeet – slipping into the back garden unnoticed. As Mark Cocker points out: 'In the UK they shout foreignness. They are bright green, they have red beaks, and they have this loud, raucous call...'

The arrival of parakeets, initially in West London gardens from the late 1960s onwards, soon attracted the attention of the media. In 1974, a reporter from the tea-time TV programme *Nationwide* visited a Mrs Vera Thompkins, who recalled the very first time she saw this exotic and unfamiliar bird outside her back window:

One came and sat on the top of the pear tree in the neighbour's garden, and I thought what a wonderful thing it would be if it came after my birds' food. And of course he did. Well then in a day or two there were two, a day or two after that there were three, and then four, and on Boxing Day there were twenty-two!

GARDEN BIRDS

The *Nationwide* report suggested that the parakeets had probably escaped from a local aviary. But in the decades that followed their unexpected arrival in the London suburbs, all sorts of urban myths arose to try to explain their origins. These included the idea, recently given a new airing in actor Michael Caine's biography *From the Elephant to Hollywood*, that they had escaped from the set of *The African Queen*, the feature film starring Humphrey Bogart and Lauren Bacall, when it was being filmed at Shepperton Studios.

Plausible though this sounds, it has never been explained how or where the birds managed to hide for almost two decades from the making of the film in the early 1950s, to their initial appearance in the late 1960s.

Another wonderful urban myth about the parakeets' origin claims that the late, great rock guitarist Jimi Hendrix kept two parakeets named Adam and Eve in his girlfriend's apartment in London's Carnaby Street. One day, in a drug-fuelled haze of misplaced compassion for these caged creatures, he is supposed to have opened a window and released them into the city streets.

The date of the story – 1969 – certainly fits with the initial arrival of the birds, but no one has ever managed to verify its truth. Even if they could, it seems highly unlikely that the entire UK population – now numbering well into the thousands – could have descended from just one pair.

A far more plausible explanation for their origin is that cage-bird dealers either deliberately or accidentally released flocks of parakeets in several locations around the London suburbs over a period of time, and that these sociable birds eventually managed to find each other and breed. Certainly in the past two decades numbers have increased very rapidly indeed, with more than 3,000 birds seen at a single roost at Esher Rugby Club, Surrey, until the trees in which they spent the night were cut down a few years ago.

Today the Ring-necked Parakeet is a familiar sight on garden bird feeders and in wooded parks throughout the London sub- urbs with small colonies of the birds spreading farther afield. They have since been recorded in many places across the coun- try, including Yorkshire, Lancashire, North and South Wales, and southern Scotland.

Despite their tropical appearance, these parakeets are well adapted to the British climate – their origins in the foothills of the Himalayas in northern India mean they can cope perfectly well with below-zero temperatures.

They have also taken to the artificial habitat of suburbia as well as any of our other garden birds. David Attenborough, who regularly sees parakeets in his leafy garden in Richmond-upon- Thames in Surrey, welcomes their presence here: 'I have to say I like them. They of course make a mess and they make a noise, but by golly they're lovely, aren't they? They're absolutely beautiful! I get up in the morning and I look out and there are six or eight parakeets, and it doesn't half gladden the heart.'

And yet the Ring-necked Parakeet's acceptance as a truly British bird is not quite complete. Their propensity to feed on fruit buds, and concerns that they might drive out native hole- nesting species such as Starlings, Jackdaws and Stock Doves, has even led to the species being placed on the pest register.

'The Urban Birder' David Lindo, who sees the parakeets every day on his local patch at Wormwood Scrubs in West London, is definitely not a fan of what he regards as alien invaders: 'I'm one of the growing number of people who don't like parakeets – I actually don't like them at all. It's probably because they're big, they're green, they've got long tails – they just don't seem to fit in this countryside to me.'

Mark Cocker takes a more measured view, for the moment at least:

> To start with they brought a little touch of the exotic, and maybe that has darkened because they've become more successful, and there are rumblings that these hole-nesting birds might start to have an effect on native species. I think we'll see changes in the response from naturalists, and we'll see changes in response by the public. But for now, I welcome them, and I watch with fascination how the bird will be treated in the twenty-first century.

*   *   *

It's no accident that the Ring-necked Parakeet and Collared Dove chose to colonise our suburban gardens rather than the wider countryside. For it was during the latter decades of the twentieth century that a revolution took place in the way we attract birds to our gardens – and at the very same time, a parallel agricultural revolution was making the wider countryside an increasingly difficult and hostile place for birds to live in.

The garden-bird revolution was born out of our growing affluence as a nation, and also from our material prosperity as individuals, which would come to define our contemporary relationship with garden birds. And it was led by bird food.

In the years since birds had first begun to come into gardens, we had fed them – when we had bothered to do so at all – on leftovers from our own table. There was one exception to this: a rather exotic addition to their diet, as environmentalist Chris Baines, who pioneered the modern concept of gardening for wildlife, recalls from his own childhood: 'When I was a little boy there was a great British tradition of trying to chop coconuts in half, and I vividly remember the fiasco of trying to hit this thing as it was skidding off the table. What you fed to birds was coconuts if you were posh, and breadcrumbs if you weren't – that was it!'

As our enthusiasm for feeding garden birds grew, those with time and money went further. By the early 1980s, when birdman and broadcaster Tony Soper was making his series *Discovering Birds* for the BBC, there was a whole host of ingenious recipes for feeding the birds. Tony himself demonstrated one of these – a kind of pudding made from high-energy ingredients – on the programme. As he now recalls, he did so in the tongue-in-cheek style of one of the pioneering TV chefs, the 'Galloping Gourmet' Graham Kerr: 'People liked the idea of cooking for birds, so if you did one of these cod recipes, with fat of some kind, and seeds, of course that's very attractive to the birds.'

But with increasing demands on their time, fewer and fewer people were cooking for themselves, let alone for the birds. Instead, they turned to a convenient, shop-bought alternative – peanuts in a red net bag. These were low-grade nuts, which had been deemed unfit for human consumption. Although they were potentially nutritious for birds, they had a drawback nobody knew about, as ornithologist Chris Whittles remembers: 'The problem with peanuts used to be that a large proportion of them coming into the birdfood trade were toxic, contaminated with aflatoxin, which is a breakdown product of a mould.'

And as Chris Whittles now recalls with wry embarrassment, when birds ate the contaminated peanuts, they were slowly poisoned: 'This used to happen even in my own garden, because I used to feed through to May, and then there would be no birds left. And knowing where I got the peanuts at the time, and knowing what I now know, by that point I'd managed to kill off all the Greenfinches in the garden!'

Ironically, Chris Whittles was one of the first people to realise the seriousness and extent of the problem, and when he set up his own bird-food business, CJ Wildbird Foods, he took great care to source his peanuts so that they did not contain the poison.

He was also, along with a handful of other pioneers, one of those who during the 1970s and 1980s began to innovate, developing high-quality products designed to mimic the food eaten by wild birds, including sunflower seeds and hearts, nyger seed (particularly loved by Goldfinches) and a wide range of fat-based products.

Indeed for the Goldfinch, one of the most beautiful of our garden birds, these new products led to a change in the species' fortunes. After a sharp decline from the mid-1970s to the mid-1980s, the Goldfinch population has bounced back rapidly. This is largely thanks to the widespread provision of high-energy seeds, and flocks of these colourful birds are now a very common sight on garden bird feeders. Its close relative the Siskin – a small, streaky finch with green, yellow and black plumage – has also benefitted from a rise in garden bird feeding, enabling it to extend its range southwards from Scotland into southern Britain. Today the Siskin is a relatively frequent visitor to many gardens, especially in late winter and early spring when supplies of natural food are at their lowest.

Other unusual species also came into our gardens, many for the first time, attracted by these increasingly sophisticated foods that quickly and efficiently deliver the energy the birds need. Today, well over one hundred different kinds of bird have been recorded coming to bird tables and feeders. Whereas we once only saw sparrows, Starlings, tits and finches, by the early twenty-first century, garden birdwatchers were enjoying such unexpected visitors as Great Spotted Woodpeckers, Nuthatches, Blackcaps and Long-tailed Tits.

The new products, stacked on supermarket shelves in bright, colourful wrappers, also proved irresistible to bird-loving shoppers. Chris Baines regards this as simply another aspect of the growing consumerism of the late twentieth century:

It's quite striking to look at how the packaging and the convenience of birdfood has tracked the way in which we've changed our own eating habits. The rise and rise of prepared meals in Marks & Spencer's is echoed by being able to buy the 'fat bar' – none of this getting fat from the butcher and melting it down and mixing it with peanuts and things – it's all there in a plastic package!

Today, feeding birds is yet another way in which we express ourselves as consumers, and even practise the art of one-upmanship, according to David Lindo:

I think a lot of people deep down do feed birds
for selfish reasons – but in a good way. They
want to say 'in my garden I get this, that and the
other – I get Bullfinches, Chaffinches… I've got
a great garden for birds – what have you got?!'
There is that competitive edge, but that's fine,
because it's benefitting the birds, whichever
way you look at it, and it's bringing nature
closer to that person as well.

It is this deeper need to reconnect with nature that underpins
our nation's vast expenditure on bird food – at least £150 million pounds a year. However, Mark Cocker sees this not just as
an expression of our consumer society, but as another way in
which we make links between ourselves and the natural world:

Day after day people provide food for the birds,
and extraordinary relationships of trust are built
up. I think it's our chance to step outside the fate
of our species, which is a terrible one – I mean
who wants to be feared by every other creature?!
And that simple, Franciscan act of giving to
birds makes us feel good about life, and
redeems us in some fundamental way.

*   *   *

Our urge to reconnect with nature through the birds in our gardens is nonetheless tempered by the fact that the garden itself is an artificial, semi-domesticated space, created by us. Jeremy Mynott is concerned that by feeding garden birds, we may be in danger of turning them into little more than 'wild pets': 'I think the wish to feed garden birds is part of a larger emotional wish to somehow make the birds dependent on us, and control the birds as part of our environment – to "decorate" the environment with birds.'

The desire for control over wild nature has always been part and parcel of gardening. We've always favoured some plants at the expense of others, and waged war on those we consider to be weeds. And in recent years the popularity of television gardening makeover programmes such as *Ground Force* has led us to regard the garden not as outside of, and separate from, our home, but as part of it – effectively an extra room.

Now, having invested time and money bringing birds into this space, we may subconsciously want to control them too – we want them to behave in ways that conform to our own moral codes. This can throw up both practical and emotional issues, as Helen Macdonald points out: 'If you put a bird table in your garden, you are creating a Sparrowhawk feeding station. It's really quite funny and distressing to realise that when a Sparrowhawk flies along the backs of suburban gardens it's just taking advantage of the wonderful feeding opportunities people have created for it.'

When this ruthless predator does pay a visit, Helen Macdonald understands people's emotional response:

GARDEN BIRDS

People get very upset about Sparrowhawks, for example, because they see their garden as an extension of their living-space. So when you look out of the window and you see a Sparrowhawk pulling a Blackbird or a pigeon to pieces on your patio, it's kind of "murder on the living-room floor". And this is why some birds are described as being mean, or evil, or villainous, because they become part of the human world.

And as Bill Oddie notes, the arrival of uninvited predators into our gardens throws into sharp relief the emotional ties we develop with the birds we feed: 'If you've got used to "your" Blue Tits, and some great big predator goes whizzing through, and basically takes that away, I think inside you're going "Aaagh! That's mine!" And you know you've lost something.'

As a result, many of us have begun to divide garden birds into two camps: on one side, our friends, and on the other, our enemies, according to Jeremy Mynott:

We project human values onto the birds, and then admire them or dislike them for those. We like the Robin because it is tame and confiding – or so it appears, in fact it's the merest cupboard love – we dislike Magpies and Starlings because we think they are noisy, rackety birds, vulgar and aggressive. These are all human characteristics.

Mark Cocker shares this view: 'The melodrama that is the garden, and our encounter with it, can lead to the introduction of moral ideas in nature, which are very unhelpful.'

He points to the way that many people view Magpies – as the arch-villain of the garden soap opera – as a case in point. 'Magpies are big, bold songbirds, with not much of a song, with a great taste for young songbirds of other species, and we really hate the fact that they eat our Blackbirds, and steal tits out of the bushes.' But Magpies are fascinating birds too – intelligent and calculating. Tim Birkhead certainly thinks so, as he wrote a book about them, *The Magpies*, in 1991:

They're confident, they're cocky, and they're incredibly smart. So they will find a Blackbird or Song Thrush nest, and if the parents mob them or chase them away, they just bide their time, and come back at a more appropriate time. And then, much to everybody's horror they butcher the offspring on the lawn in front of you.

Branded as baby-killers, there's a popular view, promulgated through lurid headlines in the tabloid newspapers and on the web, that Magpies are responsible for a decline in songbirds. Tim Birkhead utterly refutes this: 'There's no scientific evidence that Magpies have been responsible for the decrease in garden birds or songbirds. The British Trust for Ornithology was involved in a very detailed survey, we at the University of Sheffield were involved too, and from a scientific point of view there's no evidence for that.'

So, although perhaps the majority of Britons blame the Magpie for a perceived decrease in songbird populations (even though, incidentally, the populations of most garden bird species are on the rise), others admire their intelligence and tenacity. Among their impassioned proponents is David Lindo: 'Magpies I defend to the death. I've had many fights with people over them, and people saying that Magpies and Sparrowhawks are causing the decline of songbirds. Well I think we're using Magpies and Sparrowhawks as scapegoats, because we are the animal that has caused the decline of songbirds much more than them.'

When viewing the garden-bird soap opera through anthropomorphic spectacles, we are often blind to the real villains – to our own role in the drama. As well as the negative effects of modern farming, industry and transport policies on bird populations, there is another factor much closer to home. Britain's domestic cats kill fifty-five million birds every year. This has placed organisations such as the RSPB in a tricky position: do they condemn cats as 'unnatural' killers of our native birds, and risk losing cat-loving members, or do they ignore the problem? So far they have tried to occupy the middle ground, offering advice on how to minimise the carnage by keeping cats indoors at dawn and dusk, or putting a bell on them. Whether this will eventually reduce the number of birds killed by cats we shall have to wait and see.

So although our relationship with garden birds is thoroughly modern, our attitudes to individual species remain pretty traditional, resistant to change even in the face of new scientific evidence.

We have our favourites, like the Robin; our friends, like the Blue Tit; and our enemies – top of the list being the Magpie and the Sparrowhawk. And in the garden-bird family there has always been one poor relation: the House Sparrow.

* * *

The recent history of Britain's sparrows reveals not only the strength of our passion for our feathered neighbours, but also our inability as garden owners to influence their fate. David Lindo, who has lived in London for the whole of his life, remembers what the situation was like when he was growing up in the capital during the 1970s and 1980s:

As a birder I never really used to look at sparrows, and then after a while I realised they weren't around any more. I used to see them all over the place – in Hyde Park, Kensington Gardens, if you went to the cafés and sat down for a cup of tea there would be sparrows by your feet. And then all of a sudden there were none there.

The rapid decline of the House Sparrow, from the 1920s and 1930s onwards, was documented by the greatest ornithologist of the twentieth century, Max Nicholson. As a young man, in 1925, Nicholson carried out a survey of the birds of Kensington Gardens, the London park near his home. Of almost 5,000 individual birds he counted, 2,600 – more than half – were House Sparrows.

GARDEN BIRDS

In the autumn of 2000, seventy-five years after his initial survey, the ninety-six-year-old Nicholson returned to Kensington Gardens to count the birds once again. This time he found just eight sparrows – a decrease of well over 99 per cent in the intervening years. Today, a decade or so later, there are none.

Bill Oddie, who has lived in London since the 1960s, recalls seeing one famous form of interaction between human beings and sparrows: 'Every park had an old gentleman, who fed the sparrows, and he always had his arms out and a hat on, and he'd be covered in them. And you could do it too. I've got photographs from that time, but you won't find this happening now.'

In the early 1990s, people living in Britain's towns and cities began to notice that their local sparrows were rapidly disappearing. Sparrow expert Denis Summers-Smith, who has studied the species since the late 1940s, takes up the story: 'They wrote to their local newspapers, they contacted their local councillors, questions were even asked in the House of Commons – what is happening to our sparrows?'

Having been taken for granted for so long, the House Sparrow was suddenly on our radar. A nation of bird-lovers was demanding to know what was going on with their cheeky little chappy. In May 2000, a major national newspaper, the *Independent*, launched a campaign to investigate. They offered a prize of £5,000 for the first person to write a published paper in a peer-reviewed scientific journal, which explained the reasons for the sparrows' sudden decline in our towns and cities.

The answer still isn't clear, but we do know that sparrow chicks are dying in the nest of starvation due to a shortage of insect food, and even those that fledge are not surviving to maturity. Together with other factors, such as the shortage of nest-sites (due to the 'yuppification' of housing and attic conversions, causing the removal of nest-sites under eaves), this appears to have dealt a fatal blow to the urban sparrow population.

Ironically, history may be repeating itself. Having initiated the decline of House Sparrows in the 1930s, motor vehicles are once again being linked to the current catastrophic fall in numbers. Denis Summers-Smith, who when he wasn't studying sparrows was pursuing a distinguished career as an industrial chemist, believes he knows the reason why: 'The one common cause, I think, is atmospheric pollution, coming from motor vehicles.'

Summers-Smith suggests that a component added to unleaded petrol to prevent 'knocking' in engines may be killing off the insects on which the baby sparrows so depend. He also believes that other chemicals, emitted by diesel engines, may also be damaging the respiratory systems of sparrow chicks, preventing them from reaching maturity.

So although the *Independent's* prize has not yet been awarded, it seems certain that a combination of factors beyond the garden fence is responsible for the sparrow's demise. Much like the miner's Canary, our sparrows may be telling us something important about our own environment. Denis Summers-Smith certainly believes so: 'Sparrows live in our urban habitat, and if something is happening to them it is high time we knew what it is, because it may be happening to us later on.'

In August 2007, our longest-standing garden bird, once so numerous as to have been considered a pest, was put on the Red List of threatened species.

GARDEN BIRDS

*   *   *

The creation of the modern British garden gave us a new, sub-urban space, in which we forged an equally modern relationship with the birds that came to live alongside us. Garden birds are creatures of our making, and by watching and feeding them we've come to know them intimately, and drawn them deeper into our domestic and emotional lives than any other group of birds.

So it's hardly surprising that from the Robin to the Blue Tit, and the Blackbird to the House Sparrow, these are the birds with which we feel the greatest connection. But this has not always been the case: other major groups of British birds have had an equally powerful impact on our culture and history, as the next three chapters will reveal.

WATERBIRDS

Of all Britain's birds, surely the most charismatic, beautiful and fascinating are our waterbirds. From the jewel-like beauty of the Kingfisher, to the cryptically camouflaged Bittern; and from our smallest duck, the Teal, to the largest British bird, the Mute Swan, waterbirds have always had a special place in our hearts.

And, of course, our stomachs. For centuries, plump and succulent ducks, geese and swans – as well as thin and rather stringy herons, bitterns and cranes – had a central place on the British menu. First they were trapped and snared; then, with the development of effective firearms in the eighteenth and nineteenth centuries, they were shot in their tens of thousands.

For the poor, these birds provided an abundant and welcome source of protein in what otherwise would have been a dull and monotonous diet. For the rich, they provided a form of 'conspicuous consumption', enabling them to make a very public display of their vast wealth, as thousands of birds were killed to adorn the tables of outrageously wasteful royal and aristocratic feasts.

But our love of waterbirds has not always been purely gastronomic. We have always had a passion for the wild and lonely places where they choose to live: the fens and marshes, bogs and lakes, rivers and streams of lowland Britain.

For centuries these places held a strange fascination for our ancestors: flat, misty landscapes filled with the echoing sounds of vast, unseen flocks of waterfowl. These were deeply mysterious and often dangerous places for their human inhabitants, where a false step could lead to a rapid death by drowning. But they also appealed to a primeval need in the human spirit – the lure of the wild.

As time went on, we began to realise that these places could be exploited in new and different ways: by draining the water from them and using the reclaimed land to graze livestock or grow crops. And by the seventeenth century, at the dawn of the modern era, we finally had the technological means to do so.

It was when we began to covet these vast wetlands, and drain the lifeblood out of them, that Britain's waterbirds began their long, slow process of decline. One by one, the Crane and the Avocet, the Osprey and the White-tailed Eagle, the Bittern and the Great Crested Grebe, all slid towards extinction.

But at the eleventh hour, not much more than a century ago, the tide finally turned. Compassion began to triumph over greed, and instead of exploiting these birds, we chose to protect them, and their watery homes. How we came to do so is the fascinating story of Britain's waterbirds.

*   *   *

The story of how we went from exploiting waterbirds to protecting them begins more than a thousand years ago, with a holy man who simply wanted to keep warm at night; and his relationship with a very special kind of duck.

The Eider is our largest, heaviest and fastest-flying duck, weighing in at over two kilos, and flying at speeds of up to 76 kilometres per hour (47.5 miles per hour) – a world record for any species of bird in level flight. Males are stunning: at a distance they appear black and white, but when you get closer to them they reveal a subtle wash of pink on the chest, and small, moss-green patches on either side of their head.

Male Eiders also have one of the most bizarre and extraordinary sounds of any British bird: a sound described by veteran birder and broadcaster Bill Oddie as being 'like a cross between a posh lady who's heard something a bit naughty, and Frankie Howerd'. And there's no doubt that the late comedian would have been amused to hear such an accurate representation of his trademark exclamation of surprise!

But it wasn't the male Eider's sound which made it world famous, but the female Eider's plumage. Eider ducks are very different in appearance from the drakes. Their plumage is, like the females of so many species of duck, designed to help the bird remain camouflaged from predators as she incubates her precious eggs. Female Eiders are basically brown in colour, although a closer look reveals a subtle beauty to their feathering – shades of buffs, browns and blacks, in little waves known as 'vermiculations', which blend together to create a very pleasing effect.

To line her nest, the female plucks soft feathers from her own breast, into which she lays her clutch of four to six eggs.

WATERBIRDS

This down is, ounce for ounce, the warmest natural material known to man. In parts of the northern hemisphere, such as Iceland, eider down is still collected each spring. This is a form of sustainable harvest, as the duck simply replaces what has been taken by plucking more down from her breast. The down sells for up to £600 a kilo – about the same price, weight for weight, as silver. Indeed the price for a bed cover filled with top-quality eider down can, in Japan and Germany, be as much as £7,000.

The reason this product is so valuable is that each piece of down is covered in tiny 'hooks' that cling onto one another, trapping little pockets of air between them. As a result, it has the very best insulating qualities of any natural down – even better than the finest goose down.

And, of course, this extraordinary material also gave its name to a household object once found in every home in Britain: the eiderdown. In an era where duvets have replaced the traditional sheets, blankets and eiderdown in almost every British home, a new generation doesn't always make the connection between the object and its origin as the down of the Eider duck. Now that eiderdowns are rapidly going out of fashion, people do get a bit confused. Bill Oddie recalls that one young visitor to the Farne Islands pointed excitedly to the Eider ducks when he arrived, calling, 'Mummy! Daddy! Look, look – a duvet duck!'

The link between the down of the Eider and the story of bird protection in Britain goes back fourteen centuries, to a seventh-century monk, St Cuthbert. Cuthbert and his fellow monks had chosen a life of devotion and austerity, in one of the remotest, and chilliest, places in Britain: Holy Island (also known as Lindisfarne), off the Northumberland coast. They shared their home with a large population of nesting Eiders.

According to scientist Tim Birkhead, author of *The Wisdom of Birds*, St Cuthbert's fame derived partly from his ability to get so close to these wild birds:

> **St Cuthbert gained notoriety for his relationship with the Eider duck. People who went to visit him were amazed that these ducks followed him around, and this gave him a saintly appearance. What they didn't realise was that all ducks have this propensity to imprint on the first thing they see when they hatch out of the egg.**

Baby Eiders, like the young of all ducks, geese and swans, are precocial. This means that almost as soon as they hatch out from the egg they are able to leave the nest and search for food. But until they fledge, they are still under the care of their parents – often in a crèche attended by several female Eiders. As a result they have developed a mechanism of recognising their own mother almost as soon they are born: a technique known as 'imprinting'. So rather than being some kind of saintly magic, Cuthbert's apparent gift was simply the result of this particular biological adaptation, as Tim Birkhead notes: 'He must have had some Eider eggs, and the chick emerged from the shell, saw him, and thought, "You must be my mum!"'

Cuthbert was so fond of his Eiders that he passed strict laws forbidding local people from killing them, or stealing their eggs or down. This was the very first time any British bird had been given official protection, and preceded the founding of official bird-protection organisations such as the RSPB by well over a thousand years.

But did this saintly man have another, more selfish, motive for offering sanctuary to the ducks? Bill Oddie has his suspicions: 'It's possible that it was for his own warmth! He said, "I don't want anybody else taking these Eider ducks because I'm going to have a very, very, very big eiderdown"!'

Birder and cultural historian Mark Cocker broadly agrees, though he takes a more generous view of Cuthbert's wider motives for protecting the Eiders: 'I think St Cuthbert was looking after an economic asset, but was also, in that classic Christian tradition, seen as somehow transcending our own ideas of animals being fearful of man the hunter.'

Like a later saint, the thirteenth-century Francis of Assisi, Cuthbert is today linked with a series of holy men who extended God's protection to the wild creatures around them.

But whatever his motives, Cuthbert became closely associated with this species, so that even today his name is commemorated in the local name for the Eider, which is still affectionately known in Northumberland as 'Cuddy's Duck'. And he deserves to be remembered, for by protecting the Eiders he was many centuries ahead of his time. Britain's waterbirds would not be truly safe for another 1,200 years or more.

* * *

In the centuries following Cuthbert's death, Britain's waterbirds continued to thrive. And they had plenty of space in which to do so, in a very different landscape from today. Britain was, essentially, a much wetter place, as low-lying, marshy areas, both inland and along the coast, had yet to be drained. So vast areas of the country, from the Somerset Levels in the west to the Norfolk Broads in the east, were more or less permanently flooded, providing huge areas of ideal habitat for these birds to feed, breed and spend the winter. But the greatest wetland of all was that vast, marshy area covering much of East Anglia, known as the Fens.

The Fens were a huge area of low-lying land – mostly at or just above sea-level – covering much of modern Cambridgeshire, Norfolk and Lincolnshire. Apart from a few higher areas of land, such as the Isle of Ely, the whole landscape was flooded for much of the year. During the winter months, local rivers, such as the Ouse, would regularly burst their banks and spread water over the surrounding area, attracting phenomenal numbers of wintering ducks, geese and swans.

The people living in the Fens made a good living from this watery landscape: from fishing, harvesting reeds and sedges, and, of course, from catching birds.

It is almost impossible for us to imagine what the Fens must have been like before they were drained and destroyed. Perhaps only the great wetlands of the east – the Volga Delta in Russia, or Eastern Europe's Danube Delta – can give us some idea of the natural wonders of this vast wetland. Today, less than one per cent of the original Fens remains: only the National Trust reserve at Wicken Fen, and the reserves at Woodwalton and Holme Fens, are still intact. Although attempts are now being made to return the land to its original glory – notably through the ambitious Great Fen Project – these are but a pale shadow of what the Fens must have been like in their heyday, 800 or more years ago.

Environmental historian Rob Lambert paints a vivid portrait of this lost landscape:

> Wild fenland would have been a remarkably diverse and busy place; a wonderful place for the modern naturalist to enjoy. There would have been pools full of ducks and other waterfowl; there would have been reedbeds full of warblers; there would have been herons and egrets staking out the edges of pools; it would have been a very dynamic, functioning ecosystem.

In spring and summer, a myriad of waterbirds would have bred here: swans and ducks, including a rare summer visitor, the Garganey; waders, such as Avocets, Black-tailed Godwits and Ruffs; and reed-dwelling birds including Savi's Warbler, which later became extinct as a British breeding bird. More mysterious and largely unseen fenland birds would have included the Bittern, and even the tiny and elusive Baillon's Crake – a species that has long since vanished from our avifauna.

In winter, there would have been even greater numbers of birds, as wild swans from the east, geese from the far north, and ducks from all points of the compass would have gathered here to seek refuge from the bitter cold, and to find food. Mark Cocker also laments its passing: 'It was a vast wilderness, and must have been one of the most important wetlands in the whole of Europe.'

For the human inhabitants of this watery wilderness, these vast gatherings of waterbirds must have seemed like manna from heaven, for them to take as they wished. The numbers involved were simply staggering, as Mark Cocker describes: 'They would go out into the water with these walls of netting, and in a single drive they would catch up to five thousand Mallard. Five *thousand* Mallard caught in a single drive tells you that the overall population was multiples of that – was absolutely gargantuan!'

It is important to realise that this bountiful natural harvest was seen as theirs by divine right – literally a gift from God. As birder and broadcaster Tony Soper explains, our ancestors' attitudes would have been very different from those of today: 'It was the general assumption, until very recently, that the whole of Creation – apart from us – was put there for our benefit; that plants and animals were separate from people, and the relationship was one of subjugation. So if they were hungry they saw them as something to eat!'

This attitude was endorsed by no less an authority than the Bible. The Old Testament in particular included a system of beliefs defining mankind's superiority to the rest of the animal kingdom, which led to a culture memorably described by historian Keith Thomas as 'the cruelty of indifference'. Our modern sensibility – that other species share this world with us, and should be nurtured and protected for their own intrinsic value – would have largely been an alien concept to our ancestors.

In some ways it is hard to blame them for their attitude: if you were hungry, and saw such a vast wealth of food on your doorstep, it would only seem right that this had been provided by a benevolent God in order to help you survive.

What is less forgivable, especially when judged by modern standards, is the sheer excess of the royal or noble feast – the medieval equivalent of a celebrity wedding, complete with conspicuous consumption on a scale unthinkable to us even today. As Tim Birkhead notes: 'These medieval feasts were very much about how wealthy the person giving the feast was; how many birds I can have on my table tells you how powerful I am; and the number and diversity of birds that were eaten at these feasts is absolutely incredible.'

Mark Cocker points to one particular event as marking the height of this gross excess: the appointment, in 1465, of George Neville as the Archbishop of York.

Neville was very well connected – his brother Richard was a Machiavellian politician known as 'Warwick the Kingmaker', the Peter Mandelson of his day. So to show his power and status, the new archbishop held a spectacular feast at Cawood Castle, near Selby in North Yorkshire, for 2,500 of his family and friends.

At a single sitting, somewhere between 14,000 and 16,000 waterbirds were served to the diners. This included no fewer than 400 swans, 400 herons, 1,000 egrets, 200 Cranes and 200 Bitterns – more, at a single meal, than exist in the whole of Britain today. And that's not including the other foodstuffs on offer, ranging from venison and quail, through pike and bream, to 4,000 jellies and 2,000 hot custards!

This was, as Mark Cocker observes, all about a public demonstration of status and power: 'All these birds would have been an expression of your ability to access wild protein in the most exalted kind of feast that you could imagine.'

Not that it did George Neville much good: two years later he was dismissed by King Edward IV, in yet another twist to the long-running Wars of the Roses. The birds, it seemed, had given their lives in vain.

Yet surprisingly, the killing and eating of these birds on this gargantuan scale had very little effect on their overall numbers. So long as there were still large areas of fenland where they could live and breed, Britain's waterbirds continued to thrive.

But as the modern age dawned, their world was about to be turned upside down. In one of the greatest environmental catastrophes in our history, this marshy landscape would be drained of its very lifeblood – water.

Attempts to drain the Fens had begun as early as Roman times, in order to reclaim this fertile land to grow crops and graze livestock. This had continued throughout the medieval period, often under the supervision of the local monasteries. But what we would now regard as the full-scale industrial drainage of Britain's fenland took place from the early seventeenth century onwards, under the supervision of the greatest civil engineer of that era, the Dutchman Cornelius Vermuyden.

During the 1620s King Charles I commissioned Vermuyden to begin draining the Fens. By removing the water, he and his colleagues turned these vast, impenetrable wetlands into fertile agricultural land, massively increasing their value. In return, Vermuyden received a large share of what had previously been common land, much to the dismay of the local people, who found themselves dispossessed. To make things even worse, they no longer had access to the waterbirds that had always provided them with such a crucial part of their diet.

Political and economic considerations aside, we can certainly admire the dedication and ingenuity of people like Vermuyden and his men, who undertook the Herculean task of turning the water into land.

But from the point of view of the wildlife that lived there – especially the waterbirds – the loss of the Fens was a total disaster. Without their precious habitat, the number of birds began to fall rapidly; a process accelerated by advances in shooting technology, such as the development of an effective and reliable version of the breech-loading shotgun in the middle of the nineteenth century.

The results were predictable and, for Britain's waterbirds, catastrophic. Jeremy Mynott eloquently outlines the process of decline:

The draining of the Fens started us off on a rather familiar track, whereby some of the displaced birds first became local, then they became scarce, then they became rare, then endangered and finally extinct. That's because these birds are specialists: they live in these waterlands, they can't just relocate to woodland or agricultural land; they depend on the reedbeds both for nesting sites and for food.

Today, according to Rob Lambert, the Fens are but a pale shadow of what they once were: 'Wild fenland has, in the modern era, been replaced by a much more impoverished landscape; a landscape dominated by agriculture, a landscape dominated by profit. And what we have now is much bleaker, it's much less rich, it's much less complex; and most importantly, there are far fewer species of bird in that landscape.'

For Mark Cocker, the draining of the Fens is one of the greatest ecological disasters ever to occur in Britain; a disaster whose gradual, insidious nature meant that we failed to notice until it was far too late: 'The loss of the Fens is a catastrophic decline which was slow and incremental as the intensification of agriculture proceeded until today, when 99 per cent of all the Fens have gone. It was an environmental treasure of international importance – and we've lost it.'

By the middle of the nineteenth century, just two hundred years since the draining of the Fens had first begun, numbers of Britain's waterbirds had reached an all-time low. The population of once widespread wetland species, such as the Bittern, had plummeted. And the most iconic British waterbird of all, the Crane, had vanished from our wetlands altogether, along with several other species, including the Spoonbill, Avocet, Savi's Warbler and Baillon's Crake.

For another of our waterbirds, things were about to get worse – much worse. During the latter half of the nineteenth century, the Great Crested Grebe would see its fortunes nosedive, as it was driven to the very brink of extinction. Then, thanks to the efforts of a group of determined and redoubtable Victorian women, it rose Phoenix-like from the ashes, to play a vital part in the eventual Renaissance of Britain's waterbirds.

WATERBIRDS

*   *   *

Of all Britain's birds, the Great Crested Grebe has the most extraordinary and memorable courtship display. Male and female grebes pair up very early in the year, often when the lakes or gravel-pits where they live are still partly frozen.

Perhaps to make up for the chill in the air, they indulge in one of the most romantic and energetic displays in the whole of the bird world. At first they seem rather shy as they approach each other, each bird nodding its head coquettishly from side to side, extending the ruff of feathers around its face to the full. Then, as they face one another, they begin a ritualised dance, each faithfully following the movements made by its mate, as if looking into a mirror.

Occasionally the female will break off and swim away to feed; but she soon returns, and begins the performance all over again. From time to time, the male will grab a piece of water-weed or a small twig, and wave it at his mate; if she is impressed, she will do likewise, as broadcaster Kate Humble explains: 'It is so beautiful, there is something just astonishing about watching a pair of grebes getting together at the beginning of the breeding season, and saying, "Are you the one for me? Go on, prove it!" and they'll rise up out of the water going, "Look how magnificent I am – aren't I just beautiful?!"'

Finally, as a climax to the whole mating ritual, both grebes stand straight up in the water, each frantically paddling away to stay upright, in a behaviour pattern known as the 'penguin dance'. It is a truly extraordinary sight – memorably described by Kate Humble: 'To carry on the courtship they do a little dance with some weed hung beautifully over their bill. But it doesn't look like slimy old pond weed when they're doing it – it could be a tango with a rose between their teeth!'

But it wasn't the Great Crested Grebe's courtship habits that almost led to its downfall; instead it was its plumage. Unfortunately for the grebe, this attracted the attention of Victorian high-society ladies – the fashion victims of their day.

In the streets of London, Paris and New York, the plumage of birds was rapidly becoming the latest must-have fashion accessory. Women strove to outdo each other with the extravagance of their headgear: first with birds' feathers, then the birds' skins, and eventually the whole bird itself. Some women looked like walking exhibits from the Natural History Museum.

For our waterbirds, this was very bad news indeed, as Kate Humble, who recently became only the second woman president in the RSPB's long history, points out: 'Vast numbers, tens of thousands of birds, were killed every year for their plumage. Women thought, "I must have feathers in my hat, I must have a feather boa, I must have ruffs, things on my cape…" – all of which basically should have been on a bird.'

For the Great Crested Grebe, the way it had evolved to suit its watery lifestyle had turned out to be its Achilles heel. Grebes are, as a family, the most aquatic group of birds in the world. They spend virtually their entire lives on water – courting, feeding and even building a floating nest.

So, to keep themselves warm, they have developed unusually dense feathering on their body and underparts, known as 'grebe fur'. It was this that attracted the attention of the Victorian fashion designers, who used the plumage to trim and edge hats, collars and cuffs; or even made the whole thing into a muff to warm ladies' delicate hands.

As the demand for feathers and plumes grew, so more and more birds were slaughtered to supply this grisly trade – not just grebes, but all kinds of waterbirds, from home and abroad. The heron family was hit particularly hard, especially the egrets, whose snow-white plumage, including the feathery plumes from their breeding garb known as 'aigrettes', was used to decorate hats.

These feathers didn't just come from British birds, but were imported into the country from all over the world. In the fifty years from 1870 onwards, it is thought that more than 20,000 tonnes of feathers, worth an estimated £4 billion at today's prices, were brought into Britain for use in the fashion trade.

The effect on bird populations, both at home and abroad, was predictably devastating. By 1860, Great Crested Grebe numbers had fallen to fewer than one hundred breeding pairs, and the species was on the verge of following the Crane into extinction as a British bird.

But not everyone was happy with this grotesque exploitation of birds, simply to adorn the hats, coats and dresses of high-society women. Two groups of women, one in the Surrey town of Croydon, and the other in the Manchester suburb of Didsbury, decided to take a stand against this cruel and wanton slaughter. In doing so they would change the face of bird protection in Britain – and indeed the whole world – forever.

Ironically, as historian of science Helen Macdonald points out, the loudest voices raised against the killing of birds came from women from the very same social class as those they were targeting with their campaign: 'These were fairly posh women – the kind of women who otherwise would have been wearing the hats.'

Rob Lambert believes that the women's approach was firmly based on a code of moral standards – a form of compassion for the welfare of the animal kingdom that was just beginning to emerge during the late Victorian era, and which would eventually signal a wholesale shift in our attitudes towards wild creatures: 'They were imbued with a humanitarianism that captured and brought along a lot of people, and they pointed out the suffering of these birds, and said that something had to be done about it.'

So these 'ornithological suffragettes', as Rob Lambert has memorably described them, went about their campaign in a highly methodical manner. They politely but firmly persuaded their friends and neighbours to forsake the wearing of any item of bird plumage; and, having achieved this initial aim, then asked the women to join forces with them to stop the trade in its tracks. And it worked, as he points out:

> The strategies that these Victorian ladies used to campaign against the plumage trade were incredibly visionary. They held promotional afternoons, they went to church, and they noted down the names of ladies who were sitting in pews with feathers in their hats; and then on a Monday these ladies would receive a hectoring letter pointing out the suffering of the bird that had died to adorn their appearance.

As Mark Cocker notes, this must have been highly discomfiting for the recipients of such correspondence: 'Imagine receiving a letter that said: "Do you realise there are fifteen species of birds in your hat, and you have in effect killed them?"!'

Firm persuasion appeared to have the desired effect. By 1889 the Didsbury group had enough supporters to form their own society for the protection of birds, charging tuppence a time for membership. Just fifteen years later, in 1904, they received the royal seal of approval from King Edward VII, and became the Royal Society for the Protection of Birds – known today as the RSPB. The Society – now boasting more than one million members – continues to revere its women founders and celebrate their dedication to the cause of bird protection in Britain.

But in their concern for the birds' welfare, might these women have also been subconsciously thinking about their own domestic repression at the hands of their menfolk? Historian of science Helen Macdonald believes that they were:

A lot of the things they were saying were about the effects on female birds. So for example, in the horrible photographs of Australian egret colonies being slaughtered during the nesting season, the great piles of adults on the ground were always described as female birds that had been killed at the nest while they were tending their young, when in fact it would probably have been almost equal male and female.

At a time when Victorian women were firmly made to believe that their place was at home, and their role in life was to serve their husband, perhaps the plight and suffering of these birds brought home their own repressed status, and their inability to control cruelty in their own domestic sphere. So they must have felt an immense sense of liberation when they cast off these fashionable fripperies and joined together to stop this horrible trade, as Mark Cocker points out: 'I think it was part of an emancipation of women as adornments. Women saw the elaborate hat on their head as in some way a metaphor for their own social uselessness, and they didn't want to be useless; they were incredibly gifted, capable women – all the things that women are being empowered to achieve today.'

Today, in a more egalitarian world, it is perhaps hard to appreciate just how forward-thinking these women were; but when you realise that British women didn't even get the right to vote until 1918, fourteen years after the founding of the RSPB, then their achievement becomes clear.

And thanks to the efforts of these pioneering women, the Great Crested Grebe was saved – just in the nick of time. From a low point of about sixty breeding pairs the species began a slow but steady recovery. Today almost five thousand pairs of Great Crested Grebes breed in Britain, thanks in no small part to the network of artificial lakes created by gravel digging in the years following the Second World War.

The whole episode that marked the founding of the RSPB signifies a crucial turning-point in the history of our attitudes not just to waterbirds, but to all Britain's birdlife. As Rob Lambert points out: 'I think all those of us in the modern era who cherish wild birds owe these Victorian radicals who came together to form the RSPB an absolutely enormous debt of gratitude.'

During the twentieth century, Britain's waterbirds would still face threats: notably a continued loss of habitat as the drainage of their precious wetlands continued. From now on, however, our relationship would gradually shift from exploiting them to protecting them, through organisations such as the RSPB, and later the Wildfowl and Wetlands Trust. But to protect our waterbirds in the most effective way possible, we first needed to learn a little more about them.

*   *   *

With the death of the old queen in 1901, the coming to the throne of 'Bertie', the playboy prince, as King Edward VII, and the dawn of a new century, Britain began to throw off many of the outdated customs of the Victorian era. But one area proved stubbornly resistant to change – the way we studied birds. This had long been almost entirely focused on the anatomy and physiology of birds, which basically involved dissecting dead specimens in museums, as Tim Birkhead explains: 'Professional ornithology at that time was "museum ornithology" – understanding the relationships between birds, understanding their anatomy, and how that fed into their classification. The notion that anybody would go out and study wild birds was simply anathema to these museum people.'

This old-fashioned approach was still dominant, even as the Edwardian era came to an end in 1910. The idea that anything worthwhile might ever come from watching the behaviour of living birds in the field was considered absurd; and those who suggested doing so were dismissed as mere amateurs, as David Attenborough points out: 'Science was what you did in a laboratory, where you could control elements and so make worthwhile observations. Science was *not* going out and watching "dicky birds" – in the scientists' view, at least.'

But one young scientist, Julian Huxley, was deeply frustrated with these outdated attitudes, and decided to do something to change the status quo. So, in the spring of 1912, he and his brother took a fortnight's holiday in the peaceful surroundings of Tring Reservoirs in Hertfordshire, to the northwest of London. Their plan was to take a close look at the habits and behaviour of one particular waterbird – the Great Crested Grebe.

Thanks to the good ladies of the RSPB, the grebes had made something of a comeback. Being easy to observe, and with a clearly defined set of courtship behaviours, they provided the ideal subject for close and rigorous observation. In the introduction to his paper on the study, published in 1914 in the journal *British Birds*, Huxley lays out his plan, and enjoins others to follow in his footsteps: 'A notebook, some patience, and a spare fortnight in the spring. With these I not only managed to discover many unknown facts about the crested grebe, but also had the pleasantest of holidays. Go thou and do likewise.'

More than half a century later, as a young undergraduate studying zoology at Newcastle University, Tim Birkhead was deeply inspired by the sheer simplicity of Huxley's approach: 'I remember being told that Julian Huxley had done this amazing groundbreaking study on the courtship behaviour of Great Crested Grebes simply in his Easter holiday with his brother – and the idea that you could do something worthwhile in two weeks, just by being organised and focused, was a tremendous inspiration.'

Huxley crouched quietly in the reeds, using his field-glasses to observe the birds as they went about their long and intense courtship. He recorded every aspect of their behaviour in his notebook in minute detail.

But just as the women behind the RSPB might have had an ulterior motive for their obsession with cruelty towards birds, there might have been a hidden side to Huxley's passion for grebes. For despite his rigorous scientific training, he couldn't help getting deeply involved in the more intimate details of the grebes' sex life, as this passage shows: 'The hen swam to the nest, leapt onto it, and sank down in a passive attitude once more. Upon this the cock came up to the nest, jumped onto the hen's back, and they apparently paired successfully – both birds, meanwhile, uttering a special shrill, screaming cry.'

As Tim Birkhead points out, Huxley imposed his own values on the birds' behaviour:

I think it conformed to his mental image
of the way birds ought to be – i.e. monogamous.
This was very clearly a set of displays between a
male and female, working together in what he
called a 'harmonious relationship'. I find it very
bizarre that Huxley's private life was anything
but monogamous, and anything but harmonious,
and yet he imposed those values on the
birds that he studied.

Huxley had been educated at Eton where, like many young men of his time, he had crushes on some of his fellow pupils. Later, at Oxford University, he was pursued by a young woman, an experience he appears to have found simultaneously exciting yet terrifying. Helen Macdonald believes that this early confusion about his own sexuality led directly to his fascination with the courtship behaviour and sex life of the grebes.

But whatever his motives, Huxley's peculiar obsession had far-reaching consequences – not just for his own career, but for the future of science. Without ever intending to, Huxley had created a whole new branch of biology – now known as ethology, or the study of animal behaviour.

This would eventually lead to a revolution in the way we viewed the animal kingdom. No longer would people confine their studies to dissecting dead animals in darkened museums; instead, a legion of young men and women would go out into the field and observe the natural behaviour of live creatures. Without Huxley, the modern discipline of zoology – not to mention the wildlife programmes that so many of us enjoy watching on television – might not even exist.

Zoologist, author and broadcaster Desmond Morris studied as an Oxford undergraduate under Julian Huxley, and later edited a reprint of his seminal grebe study, published in 1968. He believes it was Huxley's scientific training that made all the difference. It allowed him to take his day-to-day observations of the grebes, and turn them into something far more rigorous and long-lasting: 'What was novel about Huxley's study of Great Crested Grebes wasn't anything to do with technology – all he had was a pair of binoculars and a notebook. But what he had, that other birdwatchers didn't have, was a training in zoology and an understanding of evolutionary processes.'

So unlike the average observer or amateur birdwatcher, who might have simply written down what he or she saw with no attempt to interpret its meaning, Huxley was able to offer real insight and understanding. This especially applied to the significance of what might to a casual observer seem like random movements, as this passage from his study describes: 'A pair of birds – cock and hen – suddenly approached each other, raising their necks and ruffs as they did so. Then they both began shaking their heads at each other in a peculiar and formal-looking manner.'

By analysing the birds' behaviour through the prism of his scientific training, Huxley was able to show that what might appear to be insignificant shaking and preening behaviour actually had a vital significance to the grebes' courtship, as Desmond Morris explains: 'He analyses the behaviour of these waterbirds – he doesn't just say, "Isn't that extraordinary, isn't that beautiful?" What he does is he asks about the origin and evolution of those movements, and the significance of each of the actions made by the birds.'

The grebes were doing what became known as 'displacement activity' – the use of ritualised, stylised versions of day-to-day behaviour in order to strengthen the pair-bond between the two birds. As David Attenborough notes, at times of high stress human beings often do something similar, such as scratch their head or pull their ear; and in the heightened state of courtship the grebes were simply doing the same.

Julian Huxley – later Sir Julian – would go on to become one of the century's greatest scientists, statesmen and broadcasters.

He was the first Director-General of the United Nations Educational, Scientific and Cultural Organization (UNESCO), appeared regularly as a panellist on BBC Television's *The Brains Trust* and in 1935, as Secretary of the Zoological Society of London, launched Pets' Corner at London Zoo. More controversially, he was also a leading figure in the Eugenics movement, which among its policies called for a limit to the breeding of 'genetically inferior' human beings – an approach now widely discredited, not least because of its associations with the Nazis' 'Final Solution'. On a more positive note, he also, along with Peter Scott and Max Nicholson amongst others, made huge strides in the global conservation of wildlife by setting up the World Wildlife Fund (now known simply as the WWF) in 1961. Huxley died in 1975, at the age of eighty-seven.

In many ways his greatest legacy was that he had found a way of allowing ordinary people to take part in genuine and valuable scientific study, simply by going out and carefully observing the behaviour of birds in their natural environment. And ultimately, by understanding our birds, we would be better able to protect them. In the words of David Attenborough: 'He was one of those who turned birdwatching into a science; and who recognised that in passionate, dedicated, amateur birdwatchers you had a huge scientific resource – if you could organise and mobilise it, here was a huge source of scientific data.'

* * *

By the early 1930s, thanks to Julian Huxley's pioneering work, amateur birdwatchers had begun to make a really significant contribution to science. Men like Edgar Chance, a businessman who spent his spare time observing and studying the extraordinary behaviour of the Cuckoo, and Henry Eliot Howard, who focused mainly on the breeding behaviour of the warbler family, pioneered the long tradition of what has since been described as 'scientific birdwatching'.

Another group based at Oxford University, led by Bernard Tucker and Max Nicholson, had also begun to organise bird surveys. The first of these, a national count of all Britain's heronries, took place in 1928 – and continues to be carried out by a band of enthusiastic British Trust for Ornithology (BTO) volunteers to this very day. Then in 1931, two young men, Tom Harrisson and Phil Hollom, organised an even more ambitious census: a nationwide count of Great Crested Grebes.

This aimed to discover just how far the grebe population had managed to bounce back since the dark days of the plumage trade during the late Victorian era. But this survey would have far more significance than the organisers could ever have imagined. For the third time in this story of Britain's waterbirds, the humble Great Crested Grebe would make a major contribution to our own history – this time in the very different field of social science.

This was due to the insight and imagination of one of the most fascinating characters of twentieth-century ornithology: Tom Harrisson. Once described as 'the most offending soul alive' (the title of a recent biography of Harrisson), he was a truly extraordinary man: part adventurer, part scientist, part anthropologist, part birdwatcher. According to Helen Macdonald, 'He made Lawrence of Arabia look tame.' In his early BBC career, when he worked under Tom Harrisson, the young David Attenborough recalls the difficulties of having to deal with such a mercurial character: 'He specialised in making enemies. That was what he really enjoyed doing – making a good couple of enemies, and that was a well-spent day!'

Harrisson and Hollom used every means they could to encourage ordinary birdwatchers to take part in their grebe survey. This included a press campaign through the *Daily Mail* and the BBC Home Service, which recruited no fewer than 1,300 volunteers up and down the country.

This meant they could achieve more or less blanket coverage of the grebe's breeding areas, many of which were on small lakes or ponds, which might otherwise have been forgotten or ignored. The results confirmed what was already suspected: that, with more than one thousand breeding pairs, the Great Crested Grebe had certainly succeeded in recovering from the low-point of the species' fortunes half a century earlier.

It was while he was travelling up and down the country counting grebes that Tom Harrisson had a flash of inspiration. Building on Huxley's pioneering work, he would take the techniques he was using to observe and study the birds, and apply them to another widespread species – his own. He called this new approach 'Mass-Observation'.

Mass-Observation, often simply shortened to 'M-O', was a truly revolutionary movement that changed the way we look at ourselves forever. It was born out of the febrile political atmosphere of the late 1930s, caused by mounting tensions between Fascism, Communism and western-style democracy that reached their climax with the outbreak of the Second World War. Its founders, which included poet Charles Madge and pioneering documentary-maker Humphrey Jennings, as well as Harrisson, aimed to define the British nation through the daily lives of its people. Run on a shoestring budget, and mainly staffed by volunteers, it thrived against all the odds, and eventually made a major contribution to our national and cultural heritage.

The aim of M-O, outlined in 1937 in a letter to the influential left-wing publication the *New Statesman*, was to create 'an anthropology of ourselves' – the first systematic attempt to study the British people and their daily lives.

M-O did what it said on the tin: using volunteer observers up and down the country to make close observations of ordinary people during their day-to-day lives – in their homes, at their workplaces, and during their leisure time. Cultural historian Christopher Frayling describes its wider aims: 'This was an attempt to map mass behaviour – to observe ordinary people and to understand what makes them tick. So it was a kind of live sociological survey – not just collecting statistics but actually going out and observing people.'

A key location for M-O was the industrial town of Bolton in Lancashire. Here, a team of paid investigators went out and about in the community, and wrote down people's day-to-day conversations and behaviour patterns as fully and accurately as they could. Meanwhile, a panel of volunteers all over Britain kept diaries and filled in questionnaires about their own behaviour. Interviewed in 1960, Harrisson recalled the insights he and his fellow observers gained: 'One was greatly struck, working in a place like Bolton, with the complete discrepancy between what the sort of people I was working with thought and talked about and what was being reported in the newspapers and on the BBC.'

As Christopher Frayling points out, at a time when Britain was in the grip of a very formal class system, with a widespread degree of snobbery, it was a real breakthrough to hear the voices of ordinary working people. David Attenborough agrees, and also notes the pioneering aspect of Harrisson's studies: 'It seems now absolutely obvious that you should study human beings in that kind of cold, detached, objective way. But you try to find someone who did it before!'

What was truly revolutionary about M-O was that Harrisson applied the techniques he had learned while watching and studying birds to the study of human beings. So instead of interviewing people, and asking them questions, M-O simply recorded what they were doing and saying. As Harrisson himself wryly observed: 'You don't ask a bird any questions. You don't try to interview it, do you?'

Christopher Frayling endorses this view: 'It's social research as birdwatching. You don't talk to them, you don't participate – you stand aside and watch through binoculars.'

Ironically, this technique of watching from a distance led to some criticisms of the M-O approach. After all, human beings and their lives are more complex than those of birds, and it was argued that a more flexible approach might have led to more in-depth findings. M-O was also criticised for its rather Orwellian qualities: the fact that some people felt that they were being spied on without their consent.

Nevertheless, Mass-Observation's methods are still being used today, in areas as diverse as university departments of sociology, market research, and fly-on-the-wall television documentaries. Harrisson himself went on to have a distinguished – if often stormy – career as a social anthropologist and museum curator. He lived and worked mainly in Borneo, before his premature death in a car accident, in 1976, at the age of sixty-five. Today he is more or less forgotten, perhaps as a result of a combination of his character flaws and the eclectic range of his interests. As his friend and fellow ornithologist K. E. L. Simmonds wrote after his death: 'It is one of the absurdities of our science that T. H. Harrisson – who as ornithologist, anthropologist, sociologist, biologist, museum curator, conservationist and adventurer became one of the greatest polymaths of his time – is largely unknown today.'

*   *   *

In the years between the two world wars, when Harrisson and his fellow birdwatchers were busy counting Great Crested Grebes on lakes, rivers and ponds up and down the country, Britain's waterbirds continued their comeback from their low-point a century earlier.

Every autumn millions of ducks, geese and swans – collectively known as wildfowl – continued to arrive in their millions, as they had done for centuries. Wildfowl have always found a winter refuge in Britain and Ireland, because of our position on the western edge of the vast landmass of Eurasia.

Being so close to the maritime influence of the Atlantic Ocean and its associated weather systems means that our winter climate is generally far milder than places on the same latitude farther to the east, and there are more precious hours of daylight than places to the north.

So, every autumn, wildfowl from all over the northern hemisphere – Arctic Canada, Greenland, Iceland, Scandinavia and Siberia – head towards Britain and Ireland, to take advantage of our mainly ice-free waters, which allow them to feed all season long. Under global conservation legislation, these islands are deemed to be of international importance for several species of wildfowl, including Bewick's Swan, Greenland White-fronted Goose, and Pink-footed Goose.

The same was true back in the 1920s and 1930s. But although wildfowl were no longer persecuted as they once had been, they now faced a new threat – in this increasingly crowded island, would there be enough room for them to survive? In the first few decades of the twentieth century Britain's population was rising rapidly, from just over thirty-eight million people in 1901 to forty-four million by 1921, and forty-eight million by 1941 – a rise of more than a quarter in just forty years. This was putting great pressure on remaining areas of wild habitat, as more and more land went under the plough or was covered with concrete to build roads and homes. But fortunately for Britain's waterbirds they had a champion at this crucial time, in the shape of a truly extraordinary man: Sir Peter Scott.

If the twentieth century had a patron saint of conservation, it would undoubtedly be Sir Peter Scott. He was blessed with a range of talents that must have made his contemporaries and rivals green with envy.

During his lifetime, spanning almost eighty years from 1909 to 1989, Scott's long list of achievements included being a figure-skating champion, the British gliding champion, winning a bronze medal in sailing at the 1936 Olympics, serving in the

Royal Navy during the Second World War (for which he won a Distinguished Service Cross for bravery), inventing a new way to camouflage battleships, co-founding the World Wildlife Fund, and becoming an internationally renowned wildlife artist. He also made regular appearances as the presenter of early natural history programmes on BBC radio and television.

His talent came from both his parents. His mother Kathleen was a distinguished sculptor, while his father was one of Britain's greatest national heroes, to rank with Admiral Nelson, Shakespeare and Florence Nightingale. This was the polar explorer Captain Robert Falcon Scott, or, as he was known to generations of British schoolchildren, 'Scott of the Antarctic'. Scott and his team had come second in the race to the South Pole, cruelly losing to the Norwegian explorer Roald Amundsen, and had then perished as they tried to return to the safety of their base camp. Despite – or probably because of – this heroic failure, Scott had become a byword for British pluck and bravery against all odds. Once the news of his tragic death reached Britain, his infant son Peter gained instant fame, becoming a national treasure overnight.

David Attenborough knew Sir Peter Scott well, first through their early work together at the BBC, and later as two of the key pioneers of twentieth-century conservation. His verdict on Scott's character is both perceptive and accurate: 'Peter was urbane, highly civilised, a delight to be with, always generous – but beneath he had a will of iron, a will of steel.'

This iron will was undoubtedly the result of his early upbringing, notably the loss of his father in such extraordinary, and public, circumstances. For many people, the requirement to live up to his father's fame and legend would have proved an intolerable burden. But this young man rose to meet the challenge, and despite being so prominently in the public eye, he went from achievement to achievement in what has often been described as a charmed life.

In later years, he would modestly ascribe his success, especially in the field of wildlife and conservation, to a stroke of good fortune. For as Captain Scott sat in his tent in a snowstorm, knowing that death would inevitably come, he wrote a last letter to his wife. This was eventually discovered when the bodies of Scott and his men were found the following spring. It contained the celebrated lines: 'Make the boy interested in natural history, it is better than games… they teach it at some schools.'

Kathleen Scott took her late husband at his word, and sent the young Peter to Oundle School in Northamptonshire. Here, he came under the influence of headmaster Kenneth Fisher – coincidentally the father of Scott's future friend and colleague, James Fisher. After school, he went on to read natural sciences and the history of art at Trinity College, Cambridge. Following his graduation in 1931, he lived in a lighthouse on the shores of the Wash, where he spent his time watching and painting wildfowl.

But he also pursued them in a very different way. For Peter Scott's early encounters with birds came not with a paintbrush or a pair of binoculars, but down the barrel of a gun. As a young man, Scott was a wildfowler, shooting and killing the very birds he later came to protect. Like so many conservationists of his generation, later known as the 'penitent butchers', he came to regret his early enthusiasm for wildfowling. However, he always freely admitted to his past, as in this interview carried out by the BBC just before he died, in 1989:

> I think there is an instinct within us which goes back to our forefathers, who had to kill to eat, and I think it's still there. And I'm bound to say that I passed through a period – and I hate remembering it, but I don't want to cover it up, because it's true – there was a time when I really took a great delight in successfully killing. I hate to think it was so, but it was so.

Ironically, Peter Scott's own journey, from hunting waterbirds to protecting them, mirrors in this single lifetime the change in attitudes towards these birds over our nation's history – from killing and exploitation, to protection and delight.

Scott's 'road to Damascus' moment came when he was still a young man, when he shot a Pink-footed Goose, but only managed to wound it. The bird then landed far out on the mud of the Wash – too far away for him to shoot it and put it out of its misery, but also – with soft mud between him and the bird – making it impossible for him or his dog to reach it. From that very moment, he vowed never to shoot a living creature again – and he never did.

To atone for his past life as a wildfowler, Scott decided to study ducks, geese and swans in order to better protect them. So in 1948 he founded his famous collection at Slimbridge in Gloucestershire, initially called the Severn Wildfowl Trust. This soon became the Wildfowl Trust, and is now the Wildfowl and Wetlands Trust – a name change that reflects Scott's own wider concern for the places where these waterbirds spend their lives.

At Slimbridge, for a small entrance fee the public could for the first time get close to waterbirds, not just from Britain but from all over the world. It may not seem so today, but then, as David Attenborough notes, this was a truly revolutionary approach – bringing nature and people together in such a way for the very first time: 'I think Peter pushed the boundary of how close human beings and the wild world could be, and how they could exist in harmony, absolutely cheek by jowl. Now of course it's not easy to do that with lions, but you can do it with wildfowl.'

Another friend of Scott, Desmond Morris, recalls that people were highly sceptical about this aspect of the venture: 'He built a whole zoo based purely on wildfowl. And people said at the time, "That won't last, you can't expect people just to go and see wild-fowl." But they did!'

During the following decades, millions of people flocked to Slimbridge, and the WWT went from strength to strength. Today it is the leading wetland conservation organisation in the world, with almost 200,000 members.

But Peter Scott did far more than simply establish a collection of waterbirds and show them to people. His lifelong passion for them had taught him a crucial lesson; one that would change the way we regarded the natural world forever. He was one of the very first people to truly appreciate the intimate connection between these birds and the wild places where they live. As David Attenborough recalls: 'Peter learned very early on that the environment and the animal were linked – that a bird could only exist, in the true sense of the word, in its proper environment.'

Today we call this set of connections between different species and their habitats 'ecology' – a word that has entered the mainstream of all conservation thinking. But at the time Scott's view was truly revolutionary and, thanks to his influence and connections, it eventually laid the foundations for the development of international conservation during the second half of the twentieth century and beyond. As Rob Lambert says: 'What this taught people was that there was no use protecting just the species; you had to protect the habitat in which the species lived, because the habitat and the species were interlinked.'

Following his success with Slimbridge, Peter Scott went on to create a network of nine wetland centres, in all four home nations of the United Kingdom. The last of these to be built, the London Wetland Centre, is also the most extraordinary.

This urban nature reserve in the heart of our nation's capital owes its existence to the vision of Peter Scott. In the very last picture he ever painted, he created an image of what the centre might look like – ducks, geese and swans landing amidst an urban oasis, with the London city skyline behind. Following Scott's death in 1989, four concrete reservoirs on the site at Barn Elms, alongside the river Thames, were demolished, and the site was turned into this unique centre, which finally opened to the public in May 2000.

David Attenborough, who as a West London resident is a regular visitor to the centre, believes that Peter would have been delighted with the results. And he has a vision of the difference the centre has made to the waterbirds themselves:

The most poetic thing which I treasure is that
there are birds in Siberia, if birds could talk, who
will say, 'Oh well, it's autumn now, I think the
place to go is Barn Elms.' And birds all over the
north in the autumn and the south in the spring
head for Barn Elms – they voluntarily go to the
middle of the biggest conurbation of human
beings in Europe and say, 'That's the place
to be.' And I think that's wonderful!

*　　*　　*

To the British public, however, Peter Scott's greatest fame came
via the new medium of television, as presenter of the BBC series
Look, which began broadcasting in 1955. Each week Peter and
his studio guests would broadcast live from Slimbridge, with
Peter chatting informally about whichever natural history topic
caught his eye. The series was an immediate hit with viewers,
including a teenage boy in Liverpool, Paul McCartney, who
wrote to Scott asking for 'the drawings of them ducks, if you
aren't doing anything with them'.

One episode broadcast in the late 1950s, *The Return of the
Avocet*, told the uplifting story of how one rare and beautiful
waterbird had come back from the dead. With its black-and-
white plumage, long bluish-grey legs and a slender, black,
upturned bill, the Avocet is one of the most striking yet bizarre-
looking of all our birds. The bill is the key to its extraordinary
feeding technique, in which the bird wades up to the top of its

legs in water, swishing it gently from side to side in order to grab tiny aquatic invertebrates.

Avocets may look graceful and elegant, but as Bill Oddie notes, they are also one of our most feisty and aggressive birds: 'The Avocet may appear to be the epitome of grace and elegance but it has a really nasty side! They are so belligerent – they will drive away anything else.'

Nesting Avocets will habitually harass any other bird that encroaches into their breeding territory, often chasing away birds much bigger than themselves, including ducks and geese. This means that many conservationists have an ambivalent regard for them – it's great to have them breeding on your nature reserve, but not so good if they drive every other species away!

The Avocet has an exotic, rather foreign-looking quality about it – few other birds are quite so elegant and stylish in appearance – yet it was for many centuries a fairly common British breeding bird, nesting in the East Anglian Fens in large numbers. But by the middle of the nineteenth century it had been driven to extinction in Britain, by the usual combination of per-secution and habitat loss due to extensive drainage.

The story of the Avocet's comeback is a truly extraordinary one. It came about largely by accident, as the result of Adolf Hitler's plans to invade Britain during the Second World War. Jeremy Mynott explains: 'Avocets made a dramatic return to this coun-try. It was in the late 1940s, in the aftermath of the war, when they returned to the habitat of flooded marshland on the Suffolk coast – which ironically had been created as a consequence of the war.'

A few years earlier, to combat the threat of a seaborne invasion, large areas of coastal East Anglia had been deliberately flooded by the Ministry of Defence, including farmland at a little place on the east coast of Suffolk, called Minsmere.

Soon afterwards, a wayward bomb from a firing range blew a hole in the sea wall at Havergate Island, a few miles down the coast to the south of Minsmere. Water from the tidal river flooded in, creating the ideal habitat for Avocets. Two years after the end of the war, in the spring of 1947, they returned to both Havergate and Minsmere and began to breed. This was much to the delight of a war-weary nation desperate for some good news, as Helen Macdonald notes: 'Interestingly, the Avocet wasn't seen as a refugee, it was seen ... in terms of the waves of returning servicemen – British servicemen coming back home from overseas...'

This tied in with the nation's mood of relief and celebration, as we welcomed back thousands of British soldiers who had been serving abroad. A giant sign was even drawn into the mud along the sea wall, proclaiming 'Welcome Home Avocets'. Jeremy Mynott agrees that this was a highly significant moment, not just for birds but for Britain as a whole: 'People would have responded to this return with a great sense of excitement, and also, I think, with a sense of the restitution of a natural order; and also, at a deeper level perhaps, at the repelling of an invader.'

For the RSPB, the Avocet had an even more crucial role to play. They bought the land at both sites, and turned Minsmere into their showpiece reserve, attracting more than 100,000 visitors each year. This in turn fuelled the huge rise in membership of the RSPB during the second half of the twentieth century, with the society growing from fewer than 20,000 members in the 1950s to more than one million by the turn of the millennium.

Minsmere also paved the way for a whole new approach to

conservation: the creation of habitats especially designed to appeal to rare breeding birds. The reserve's warden, H. E. (Bert) Axell, was a truly visionary man, who knew that to keep Avocets breeding at Minsmere he would have to make the place irresistible to them. The habitat he created, a series of shallow brackish lagoons and small islands known as 'The Scrape', is still the centrepiece of the reserve today – and still supports breeding Avocets, along with many other nesting waterbirds.

Since then, Avocets have managed to extend their range to many parts of Britain, and today more than 1,500 pairs nest at almost seventy sites up and down the country, although breeding success can often be low because of predation by crows and foxes. And several thousand Avocets, many coming from the Netherlands, spend the winter months on our south coast harbours and estuaries.

The bird itself has become a classic symbol of conservation success. So when it came to choosing a logo for the RSPB, what could be more appropriate than this beautiful waterbird, which by then had become an icon of the bird protection movement? As Helen Macdonald points out, it was an inspired decision:

I think the RSPB's choice of the Avocet as a symbol was very clever. It was strange, it was glamorous, it was a bird that most people hadn't seen, but it was a bird that most people wanted to see. And it was a bird that you could only see if you joined the RSPB and went to one of their reserves!

The choice of the Avocet – in a stylish logo designed by the renowned bird artist Robert Gillmor – was a pragmatic one, too: conveniently, in the days before colour printing, it was black and white!

* * *

Meanwhile, five hundred miles to the north, in the forests of Speyside in the remote highlands of Scotland, another rare waterbird was also about to make a dramatic comeback.

The Osprey is one of the most widespread birds of prey in the world. Found in all seven continents apart from Antarctica, it exists solely on a diet of fish, which it catches by flying low over the surface of the water and grabbing its unsuspecting prey with its huge claws.

It was this dietary preference for fish that led to the Osprey's downfall in Britain. Back in the Middle Ages, when Britain was still a Catholic country, eating meat was forbidden on Fridays. So every large house would have had its own fishpond, where fish could be bred and harvested. And as Osprey expert Roy Dennis points out, this proved to be very attractive to this fish-eating predator: 'If you provide a fishpond – whether you did it in the Middle Ages or you do now – all the Ospreys go straight to it.'

For the Osprey, taking advantage of an easy supply of food was fruitful in the short term, but would eventually lead to its demise. So even by the time the Victorians were blasting away with shotguns at any bird with a hooked beak and sharp claws, the Osprey was already a very rare bird. And unfortunately, as it got rarer, so museums and private collectors wanted an Osprey skin or its eggs – or both. This, of course, hastened its decline.

As a result, by the opening decades of the twentieth century the Osprey had been driven to the very edge of extinction as a British breeding bird. It is often said that it actually went extinct in the years between the two world wars, but Roy Dennis believes that one or two pairs managed to hang on in the remotest parts of the Scottish Highlands, or that occasional birds dropped in on the way north from their winter quarters in Africa to their Scandinavian breeding grounds, and stayed around to breed.

When a pair of Ospreys returned to nest in the spring of 1954 in Loch Garten in the Spey Valley, the news had to be kept as secret as possible to try to prevent the nest being robbed and the eggs taken. So the Director of RSPB Scotland, George Waterston, did all he could to guard the nest, as Rob Lambert explains: 'He set up what has become known as "Operation Osprey", but which was, in effect, the militarisation of a natural landscape.'

This went right back to Waterston's wartime experiences. He had spent several years as a prisoner-of-war in a camp in Bavaria, and Helen Macdonald believes this had a profound influence on the way he went about safeguarding the nesting birds now in his care:

When he was charged with looking after the Osprey nest he spent a lot of time recreating a prisoner–of–war camp around it. He had barbed wire, he had watchers who would peer down the sights of .22 rifles all night just in case anyone came along to steal the eggs; he

really recapitulated his wartime experiences protecting these birds.

Yet despite all his efforts, from time to time the nest still got robbed, with one enterprising thief even replacing the clutch of Osprey eggs with hens' eggs covered in boot polish to try to fool the nest guards, as Waterston revealed when he appeared on Peter Scott's *Look* programme.

Waterston and his colleagues were at their wits' end – and then, with a flash of inspiration that would change the way we British watch birds forever, Waterston took a brave, momentous and far-reaching decision. Instead of keeping the nest site secret, he would not only tell the public where it was, but invite them to come and visit. As Rob Lambert points out, the overwhelming response to this suggestion was one of outrage and disbelief: 'There was absolute horror in the mainstream conservation movement at the time. The nest of any rare breeding bird had to be kept secret – and Waterston was essentially saying the absolute opposite. People thought he was mad – that he was just crazy.'

And yet, as it turned out, the sceptics were wrong, and Waterston's instincts were proved absolutely right. In 1959, the first summer the public were invited to come and see the Ospreys, no fewer than 14,000 visitors made the long trek north to do so.

It was then that the method behind Waterston's apparent madness became clear. The constant presence of so many people, as well as interest from the media, meant that any would-be nest-robber would have to get past not just a few dedicated guards, but potentially hundreds of pairs of eyes. Mark Cocker believes this was the key to the scheme's success: 'In a curious way the public in some sense did the job of the nest guardians, because they were present day-in and day-out during the breeding season. The public were always on hand.'

Or as Bill Oddie puts it, it was like the house that doesn't get burgled because there are always people there.

It was also a brilliant bit of public relations – the Ospreys became overnight celebrities, their annual return reported in newspapers, on the radio and on television; and the success (and occasional failure) of their breeding attempts given plenty of media coverage. This had a profound effect on the local economy: over subsequent years local businesses, and even whole villages, would turn the Osprey into a brand to market their goods and services.

But not everyone was a fan of this new approach. As a young man, Jeremy Mynott recalls making the long and arduous journey north to Speyside to see his first Ospreys. Despite his eager anticipation, he ended up feeling rather short-changed:

My experience was probably untypical, in that I was terribly disappointed. When I got near to the site I walked down the boardwalk, and I entered a hide that was jammed with people. I was pushed in front of a mighty telescope, which was trained on a distant tree, swathed with barbed wire – and all I saw was the top of an Osprey's head. It was rather like going into an armed camp, or a heavily fortified zoo, and it was a complete anti-climax.

Mynott did what many other people have done before and since – he explored other lochs in Speyside until he found his own Ospreys, which he could enjoy in peace and solitude.

But even though it didn't appeal to everyone, Operation Osprey was, for most people, the ideal way to encounter these beautiful birds. In the half-century that has passed since that first summer of 1959, well over two million visitors have made the pilgrimage to see successive generations of breeding Ospreys, making them the most observed dynasty of birds anywhere in the world.

And even today, people continue to make the pilgrimage to Speyside in their thousands. This is despite the fact the Osprey has enjoyed a boom in numbers, and about 200 pairs of this iconic raptor breed in Scotland, with a few pairs in parts of England and Wales. The continued popularity of Loch Garten must surely be because the site itself offers the complete 'Osprey experience', as Bill Oddie describes:

I think it's because they get a bit of a show there – they know they're going to get a video feed [from CCTV cameras trained on the birds' nest], there are people who can tell them all about the Ospreys, they can join the RSPB, they can buy a fluffy Osprey – you press them and they call! It's show business – and it works very well!

WATERBIRDS

Once the RSPB realised just how successful bringing birds and people together could be, they rolled it out all over the country, creating a whole new way of watching birds, one aspect of what is known today as 'eco-tourism'. This has allowed tens of thousands of people to get great views of various different species of rare breeding bird, including Peregrine Falcons, Montagu's Harriers and Golden Eagles, at watchpoints staffed by local experts, with powerful telescopes trained on a particular nest.

These schemes even operate in our city centres, such as London and Manchester, where shoppers and passers-by can enjoy close-up views of nesting Peregrines on the giant video screens usually used to screen football matches. But the big birds of prey are still the biggest draw, and just as we now associate Speyside and Loch Garten with Ospreys, so we now associate the Isle of Mull with another great wild bird experience – White-tailed Eagles.

*   *   *

For children all over Britain, the Isle of Mull means just one thing – its main town of Tobermory is home of the popular children's TV series *Balamory*. Today a steady stream of families travels to the island each year, keen to see the various locations where the series was filmed.

But the Isle of Mull is also home to another major tourist attraction: Britain's biggest bird of prey, the White-tailed Eagle, also commonly known as the Sea Eagle. With a wingspan of about three metres – considerably wider than a man's arms – and standing as tall as a large dog, the White-tailed Eagle is the big daddy of British waterbirds.

Not far off a metre in length, and weighing up to five and a half kilograms (12 lbs) the White-tailed Eagle is the largest of our birds of prey – even larger than a Golden Eagle. Like other species of sea eagle around the world, it is rather vulture-like in appearance, with broad wings, a large pale head, a huge yellow bill, and – in the adult bird at least – a snow-white tail. It has been described as 'a flying barn door', and when you first see one the experience can be more than a little overwhelming, as Kate Humble recalls from her own first sighting on the Isle of Mull: 'I can tell you that the first time you see one you will never forget it – probably like your first kiss! They have a haughtiness, there's something kind of terrifying about the look of them.'

For a true sense of scale, when the eagles are mobbed by local Hooded Crows or Ravens – which themselves are pretty large – you realise just what a giant of a bird this is.

Like so many of our birds of prey, the history of White-tailed Eagles in Britain is one of persecution, decline and, in this case, extinction. Back in the Middle Ages the species would have been a common sight, not just in Scotland but across most of England, Wales and Ireland. Even in the middle of the nineteenth century they could still be found breeding around the coasts and islands of Scotland and parts of Ireland.

But by the end of the Victorian era, the White-tailed Eagle's days were numbered. Shot on sight by gamekeepers and sheep farmers, and then pursued by collectors eager to lay their hands on such a rare bird and its eggs, the eagle finally became extinct in Britain in 1916.

Unlike the Osprey, the White-tailed Eagle did not manage on its own to return here to breed. Instead, it was given a helping hand by us, in what eventually became the first successful rein-troduction scheme of any British breeding bird. At first, how-ever, things did not quite go to plan. The earliest attempts to reintroduce the eagles, in the Scottish Highlands in 1959, and on Fair Isle, in 1968, both failed, with the birds either dying or flying away soon after they were released.

But valuable lessons were learned during these unsuccessful attempts, and from the mid-1970s onwards a dedicated reintro-duction scheme began on the Isle of Rum in the Inner Hebrides, off Scotland's west coast. Over the following decade, almost a hundred young eagles were brought to Scotland from Norway (where the population was still thriving) and released on Rum; with more being let go later on, at other sites in the west of Scotland.

Being such a long-lived bird, it took plenty of time before the eagles would settle down and breed. So it was not until the spring of 1985 that a pair bred successfully on the Isle of Mull, follow-ing which more and more managed to establish a foothold in the region. By 2009 a new record of forty-six pairs bred, with a fur-ther scheme launched to release young eagles on the east coast of Scotland, in Fife.

Today the White-tailed Eagles attract thousands of visitors to Mull, bringing more than £1 million a year into the local economy. They have even become television stars, thanks to being featured on the BBC's *Springwatch*. But some people, including Rob Lambert, are not entirely comfortable with these birds being turned into tourist attractions: 'It is still a way of using nature. There's no escape from the fact that we are using the Ospreys and the White-tailed Eagles to generate money.

The fact that these birds have a financial value is something that sits ill with many people.'

Even though this 'use' of birds is far more benevolent than the exploitation that took place in the distant past, our intervention in their lives still generates controversy. Recent proposals to release White-tailed Eagles into parts of East Anglia have provoked passionate views on both sides of the debate.

Some local people have welcomed the scheme, pointing to the extra visitors it is likely to attract, especially during the autumn and winter months outside the peak tourist season, creating a boom for local shops, cafés and bed-and-breakfast establishments. Others, especially farmers and landowners, have strongly opposed their release, claiming that eagles will take young lambs and also potentially harm local wildlife, including breeding colonies of terns along the coast, and nesting Bitterns and other waterbirds.

And while the RSPB have pointed to the sea-change in attitudes on the Isle of Mull, where initial suspicion and hostility have given way to delight at the birds' major contribution to the local economy, other statutory bodies, such as Natural England, have been more cautious. For the time being the scheme has been put on hold.

For Roy Dennis, who as warden on Fair Isle in the 1960s was involved in one of the early release schemes, this has been deeply frustrating: 'The disappointing thing was that I think many people thought that as soon as we had twenty pairs of eagles breeding in the Hebrides – in Skye and Mull – the job was done. Whereas others of us felt the job is not done until we have them breeding back all the way from the Channel coast to Shetland.'

As President of the RSPB, Kate Humble shares his vision: 'I think if we had big birds of prey such as White-tailed Eagles back in England, rather than just in Scotland, it would be something we could all feel really proud of – that we have looked after our countryside well enough to support a beast like that.'

Other observers, including Jeremy Mynott, take a more cautious view, wondering whether our conservation bodies might have gone a little too far in their promotion of such reintroduction schemes:

The cynical view is that this is done in the name of biodiversity, but little attention is paid to birds like the Spotted Flycatcher, the Corn Bunting, the Tree Sparrow, the Willow Tit – all of which are equally endangered, but aren't such good box-office. So one begins to wonder if the societies are promoting the interest of the Sea Eagle, or is the Sea Eagle promoting the interest of the societies?

No doubt the debate over the role we have played – and continue to play – in these birds' comeback will continue. But one thing cannot be denied – just how far the bird protection movement has come since the days when women spied on each other in church to stop grebes being turned into fashion accessories.

Today, Britain's waterbirds are thriving. From Avocets to Ospreys, White-tailed Eagles to Bitterns and, of course, Great Crested Grebes, their populations are mostly on the rise. And despite continued pressures on their habitats, and the growing demand for water itself, we continue to restore wetlands – and even create new ones from scratch – in a process known, rather romantically, as 'rewilding'.

Now, deep in the heart of the West Country, another lost waterbird is being brought back from the dead. It is one of the rarest and most iconic British birds of all – the Crane.

*   *   *

Cranes are truly amazing birds. Our tallest bird, at a metre and a half high, they have been compared to the musician Jarvis Cocker (by Kate Humble) and the comedian John Cleese (by Bill Oddie). They are also deeply ingrained in our history and culture. They have given their name to places all over Britain – such as Cranfield, Cranleigh and the fictional Victorian town of Cranford, made famous by the recent TV adaptation of Elizabeth Gaskell's novel. And they have also, of course, given their name to the huge metal structures that tower over our city centres – industrial cranes were named after the bird, not the other way around.

Cranes also play an important part in cultures all over the northern hemisphere, where their annual return each spring signifies the coming of the new season, and the renewal of life for the land and its people. Yet for most of the past three hundred years, since the draining of the Fens, Cranes have been missing from the British scene, having finally disappeared as a breeding bird some time during the sixteenth or seventeenth centuries – the result of habitat loss and persecution.

Now, though, Cranes are set to return. Once again, as with the White-tailed Eagle, this is happening because we have decided to give them a helping hand. In an ambitious reintroduction scheme, run by conservation bodies including the RSPB and WWT, young cranes have been released at a secret site on the Somerset Levels.

If these birds manage to survive threats such as predation by foxes, colliding with electricity power lines, and food shortages caused by cold winters, they will soon be flying free over the home of King Arthur – the ancient land of Avalon. For Mark Cocker, this represents a very special return: 'If we've got space for a bird that stands as tall as many of our children, if we've got room for a bird with a wingspan of over two metres, in this intensely crowded island, it's a symbol of hope for all of us.'

But welcome though the sight of Cranes flying over the Somerset Levels will be, they won't be the very first to return to Britain. For in a remote corner of Norfolk, 250 miles to the east, the Cranes have already made a comeback. And what is truly remarkable is that they did it without our help.

Back in the early 1980s, a tiny handful of Cranes turned up in the far northeast of Norfolk, at a place called Hickling Broad – ironically the very same location where wild Cranes had last been recorded breeding in Norfolk back in the 1540s. They stayed, and then bred; and gradually, over the following three decades, numbers built to a current population of about eight breeding pairs. Meanwhile the species has begun to expand south and westwards, with Cranes recently breeding inland in Suffolk, and attempting to breed at other sites around the country.

For Mark Cocker, who lives only a few miles from Hickling and the Cranes, their return is much more than a mere footnote in the history of ornithology. Indeed, he regards it as a symbol of the very nature of our deep and longstanding relationship with these extraordinary birds: 'I think the wonderful thing about this is that those Cranes did it on their own. They surprise us by achieving a restoration in this country without ourselves, and I think it's proof that we aren't in charge necessarily.'

Jeremy Mynott, who lives just across the border in Suffolk, agrees: 'I'm excited to see Cranes in the places I see them in East Anglia, and I'm excited particularly because I know about the history of their return. The fact that they found their own way back seems to me a very important point.'

Mark Cocker also believes that we can learn an important lesson in humility from the Cranes' comeback: 'The danger with conservation is that it reinforces that older idea that we are always the ones that arbitrate what happens in our landscape; and what the Cranes are a symbol of is that sometimes nature can do it without us – we aren't really always in control!'

Whatever your feelings about the Crane reintroduction project, surely no one can deny that the presence of this iconic species as a British breeding bird is a worthy symbol of the continued success of bird protection, and a symbol of hope for the future of Britain's waterbirds.

SEABIRDS

B ritain is an island nation. The sea is in our history and in our blood. From childhood summer holidays by the seaside to our long and noble seafaring tradition, the British have always had a very special connection with the sea.

For centuries, Britons have travelled the world's vast oceans, as fishermen, explorers and traders. This brought us into direct contact with seabirds, both on the high seas and around our coasts. Gulls and terns, auks and skuas, petrels and shearwaters, would all have been familiar birds to many of our ancestors.

Coastal communities established deep and long-lasting relationships with these birds, living off their meat, their eggs and a host of other vital commodities. Even as late as the middle of the twentieth century seabirds were still being exploited for food.

Our long-term exploitation of seabirds is partly based on their apparent abundance. But it also stems from the long Christian tradition of making use of any of God's creatures – especially such fat and tasty ones – for our own ends, as

SEABIRDS

environmental historian Rob Lambert points out: 'There was a sense that this was something given to us by bountiful providence, and it would be wasteful not to use them.'

Through our history, though, seabirds have provided far more for us than such utilitarian needs. They have featured in our greatest literature, and in high fashion; they transformed Victorian agriculture, and created family fortunes. It is hard to overstate just how central a role seabirds have played in the lives of the people of these islands, from prehistoric times until the beginning of the twentieth century.

But in the past hundred years or so, as our fishing and shipbuilding industries have declined, and our navy has shrunk in size, our nation has gradually become more and more removed from its seafaring past. We don't even go on holiday to the seaside as often as we used to, thanks to the rapid growth of foreign travel during the post-war era. As this has happened, seabirds, too, have receded from our daily lives. So for how much longer will they continue to shape our nation's history and culture?

The story of our relationship with seabirds is an ancient and turbulent one, as ancient and turbulent as our relationship with the sea itself. It is a dramatic, exciting and largely untold chapter in the history of our rise and fall as a seafaring people.

*   *   *

Of all our birds, seabirds are the most enigmatic, the most remote from our daily lives. And yet they hold a special magic for many of us, as birder and author Mark Cocker explains: 'There is something remarkable, wonderful and extraordinary about seabirds.

I think it's to do with their sense of mystery.' Jeremy Mynott, author of *Birdscapes*, agrees: 'Birds that inhabit the sea acquire something of the charisma of the sea.'

As with so many birds, this charisma isn't purely visual, but also aural. Its appeal is almost otherworldly, as the former Poet Laureate Andrew Motion notes: 'A lot of them make a noise that sounds like something from the other side of the world that we know… extremely lonely, extremely beautiful, with a kind of forlornness about it.' Much of this wild magic – the quality that makes so many people regard seabirds as special – comes from the way they live their lives, a lifestyle so utterly different from our own terrestrial existence. For seabirds truly belong at sea, and the great expanses of open ocean are where many spend the vast majority of their time.

Of course all seabirds must come to land for a short period each year, to breed – even the most pelagic of creatures cannot lay its eggs on the surface of the ocean. But in most cases they only return to land for as brief a period as necessary; usually arriving back between March and May, and staying until July or August, when their chicks are old enough to leave the land and venture out to sea – their true home. Even when they are breeding, many adult seabirds still spend most of their time at sea, catching food for their mate or their young, and only returning to land for short periods in order to deliver their catch.

Once they have carried out their parental duties – laying and incubating eggs, and feeding and fledging their young – most seabirds head back out to the open ocean, where they spend the rest of the year. In many cases we have no idea where they go – all we know is that they are somewhere out at sea.

SEABIRDS

Another reason why as a nation we are so passionate about seabirds is that the British Isles are home to some of the greatest seabird colonies anywhere in the world. This is partly due to our position on the edge of the vast Eurasian landmass, next to the Atlantic Ocean; partly to the abundance of food in our surrounding seas; but most of all, to our 12,000 miles of rocky coastline and numerous offshore islands. Seabird expert Roy Dennis believes that these factors combine to create one of the greatest of all our natural wonders: 'Because of the North Atlantic Drift, and the continental shelf, and our rich seas, our seabirds are spectacular – this is really our equivalent of the Serengeti.'

We may not always appreciate the international importance of this vast array of life. Some seven million seabirds, of two dozen different species, nest on and around the British and Irish coasts. These include well over 75 per cent of the world's Manx Shearwaters, about 70 per cent of the world's Northern Gannets, and at least 60 per cent of the world's Great Skuas. Along with Fulmars and Kittiwakes, Guillemots and Razorbills, and everyone's favourite, the Puffin, these provide a feast for all the senses, as Rob Lambert, who has visited many of our finest seabird colonies, recalls: 'We do have these phenomenal seabird cities on our towering sea cliffs. They're bustling with activity, and a marvellous smell wafts up, which bowls people over as they first come to the edge of the cliff.'

Mark Cocker is also bowled over, by the sheer numbers of the birds themselves: 'One can probably see, at any one time, ten to one hundred thousand birds at every moment of the day – it's a kind of overwhelming abundance of life, and that's part of the British landscape.'

Yet today, when most of us live away from the coast in towns and cities far from these extraordinary spectacles, these amazing natural wonders are largely out of sight and out of mind. But it was the sheer abundance of our seabird colonies that originally made them so important and irresistible to our ancestors. That story starts on the remotest group of islands in the whole of the British Isles – St Kilda.

*　　*　　*

St Kilda – the little cluster of islands, stacks and rocks that together make up this remote and magical archipelago – is truly one of the world's most extraordinary places. Lying in the north-eastern Atlantic Ocean, some forty miles north-west of the islands of North Uist and Benbecula in the Outer Hebrides, it is the most remote and isolated place in the whole of the British Isles. Its huge cliffs and stacks, some rising straight up from the sea to more than 400 metres in height, make a visit to St Kilda a truly awe-inspiring experience. Donald Murray, an author and poet who has made a special study of St Kilda, compares it to a mythical lost kingdom: 'It's a place that looms out of nowhere; you've got all this empty ocean, and there it is – Atlantis.'

St Kilda is also one of just two dozen places in the world that has been given dual World Heritage status by the cultural organisation UNESCO – granted both for its natural heritage and its cultural and historical importance. Today, the islands are uninhabited, apart from a few seasonal visitors such as scientists, naturalists and military personnel.

Every summer about a million seabirds come ashore to these

rocky outcrops to breed. But for centuries an extraordinary island race also lived here – the men and women known as 'the bird people' of St Kilda. They earned that name because their population was largely sustained, for hundreds of years, by seabirds, as Mark Cocker explains:

The most remarkable hunter-gatherer community in Britain was the inhabitants of St Kilda – a small, Gaelic-speaking community that lived in crofts, on the edge of this huge mountain on the island of Hirta. Essentially their entire lives were bound up with what they could harvest of wild birds from the cliffs and ledges around this incredible set of islands.

The people of St Kilda looked to seabirds to meet almost all of their subsistence needs, until well into the twentieth century. They ate the flesh of the birds, of course; but they also used the feathers for pillows, and turned the skins into very short-lived shoes. The oil – mainly from the young Fulmar (a gull-like bird from the petrel family) – provided fuel for heating and lighting, at a time when fossil fuels were yet to be discovered. The islanders even derived some of their medicine from that same oil.

But the St Kildans faced a problem: seabirds only come ashore to breed for a few months every spring and summer – yet people needed to eat the bird all year round. So they buried the seabirds' eggs in ash; and dried the birds themselves using an ingenious construction called a 'cleit'.

Cleits, hundreds of which can still be seen on the mountain-side of the main island of Hirta, were small stone huts, not much taller than a man. They were constructed so that the air could enter through the gaps in the stones, but the rain was kept out. By this method, the carcasses of Puffins and Fulmars were 'air-dried', into what Mark Cocker likens to a type of 'biltong' (the South African version of dried beef). However, as the seabird enthusiast James Fisher perceptively wrote, 'It was a race between desiccation and decay as to whether the birds would be palatable.'

We might think it bizarre that this remote island race chose to eat seabirds rather than fish, which presumably were just as abundant then in the waters around St Kilda as they are today. But fishing presented three major problems. First, it was highly unpredictable: a day might be wasted searching for shoals of fish that were elsewhere, and the fishermen would return empty-handed. Second, the volatile nature of the local weather meant that any boat might either be suddenly becalmed, or worse still, sink in a storm, bringing death to all on board. This small community would never recover from the loss of so many men. And finally, the islands had no good natural harbour, so getting on and off boats was (and remains today) a very tricky process.

So, instead of eating fish – which in any case, according to Donald Murray, they found bland and rather unpalatable – the St Kildans preferred a diet of fish-eating birds; either fresh or dried, depending on the time of year.

Their diet was mainly Puffins and Gannets. In a logical division of labour, Puffins were mainly collected by the women, from their burrows on the island of Dun, just off the main island of Hirta; while Gannets were taken by the men from the cliffs of the neighbouring island of Boreray, which is home to the world's largest Gannet colony – more than 60,000 breeding pairs.

The young Gannet, also known as the guga, was particularly prized for its distinctive flavour; and even today the men of the community of Ness, on the Isle of Lewis in the Outer Hebrides, still go on an annual 'guga hunt' to the island of Sula Sgeir, a remote lump of rock in the Atlantic to the northeast of St Kilda.

Donald Murray, who as a 'man of Ness' himself has had the privilege of accompanying the guga hunt (and wrote about it in his book *The Guga Hunters*) was brought up on the taste of this local delicacy: 'I would describe guga as the food of the gods – there's something wonderful about it. Mainlanders would probably deplore the taste – I've heard it described as tasting like chamois-leather dipped in oil! I think it tastes like salt-mackerel-flavoured chicken!'

For the people of St Kilda this diet, though perhaps rather monotonous at times, was clearly a reliable one. And it proved manageable for the birds, too: although thousands of seabirds were killed each year, this appears to have had little or no effect on their long-term populations. The islanders only took what they needed to survive, and in any case the community rarely numbered much more than one hundred or so people in all. 'None of the species which they harvested ever went extinct,' explains Mark Cocker, praising the sustainable nature of the St Kildans' relationship with seabirds: 'In a curious way they were custodi-ans – they had a deep impulse to preserve the goose that laid the golden egg – and they did.'

But even though their way of life had lasted for hundreds, perhaps even thousands, of years, the modern world ultimately encroached on St Kilda. First, the cruise ships came, bringing regular visitors, with a predictable effect on the islands' economy. As the tourists disembarked, the islanders would approach them with souvenirs such as sheepskins, knitted gloves and tweeds – a lot easier, more profitable, and far less dangerous than climbing on cliffs to hunt seabirds.

Then a series of disasters struck this remote island community. First, in 1912, there were severe food shortages, followed in 1913 by an outbreak of influenza that killed off many islanders, including several children. The coming of the First World War in 1914 led to the departure of many of the islands' younger menfolk – some of whom were killed in action, while others, having seen what the outside world had to offer, chose not to return.

As a result the hunter-gatherer tradition, that had sustained the bird people for so long, had been fatally undermined, and their unique lifestyle was doomed. In 1930, the remaining population of just thirty-six islanders made the decision to evacuate, and on 29 August of that year, they left for the last time, abandoning St Kilda to the birds.

*   *   *

It was only the remoteness of St Kilda that allowed the bird people's culture to survive for so long. Archaeological evidence shows that in prehistoric times there were similar communities dotted all around the coasts and islands of the North Atlantic. But these had given up the hunter-gatherer lifestyle many centuries earlier, as it became easier to farm the land, or to trade with other communities.

Nevertheless, our connection with the sea continued, albeit in a very different way. So those Britons who went out to sea to make their living as fishermen and seafarers began to encounter seabirds in their true element – the open ocean. And in the southern oceans, far from home, one bird in particular made a deep and lasting impression on them: the albatross.

The world's two dozen or so species of albatross are the largest, heaviest and most magnificent of all seabirds. They range in size from the smaller 'mollymawks' such as the Black-browed Albatross (though 'small' is a relative term for a bird with a wingspan of more than two metres) to the mighty Wandering Albatross, whose wingspan of three and a half metres is the largest of any bird in the world.

As its name suggests, outside the breeding season (and even during it) the Wandering Albatross flies the vast southern oceans searching for fish; either to eat, or to take back to its single youngster. David Attenborough has travelled across these empty oceans, and understands just how memorable it would have been for these early sailors to encounter one of these majestic birds, so far from home: 'You're sailing, and suddenly one of these magnificent birds appears around you with that huge wingspan; and it appears out of the sky, and doesn't move its wings – just tilts and glides, exploiting the upcurrents from the surface of the sea, and then it's off again...'

Seabird enthusiast Roy Dennis is also filled with awe for these incredible creatures:

All those explorers who set off from Britain on sailing boats going round the world, in these vast areas where they saw nothing – then suddenly this incredible bird appeared on the

horizon, and came up beside their boat and
followed them through the storms. And they
must have felt a real attachment to the albatross,
and they would have come home and told
people about this incredible bird that
tracked the oceans with them.

This mysterious tendency for the albatross to track sailing ves-
sels gave rise to the pivotal scene in *The Rime of the Ancient
Mariner* by Samuel Taylor Coleridge, a poem that has entrenched
the albatross in our popular culture. First published in 1798,
Coleridge's epic work has become one of the best-known, and
most-quoted, poems in the English language, despite its great
length. The poem traces the tale of a seaman, his life-changing
encounter with an albatross, and its terrible consequences.

The mariner's ship is blown off course in a huge storm, ending up
in the icy wastes of Antarctica. Then, miraculously, an albatross appears:

At length did cross an albatross,
Through the fog it came;
As if it had been a Christian soul,
We hailed it in God's name.

The introduction of a religious element into the poem at this
stage is a very deliberate one, as cultural historian Christopher
Frayling points out: 'It's a symbol of whiteness, of conscience, of
souls, of Christianity. And it's big – like an angel. It's more than
a bird – it's a flying symbol.'

SEABIRDS

This enigmatic bird leads the ship back into warmer waters, saving the sailors from certain death. Then, inexplicably, the mariner takes aim and shoots the bird with his crossbow. His shipmates are, quite understandably, horrified; not simply because he has killed a bird, but because of what that bird symbolises, as Mark Cocker explains: 'One of the common pieces of folklore in all maritime, sea-going communities was that the souls of lost mariners entered into the bodies of seabirds such as petrels, shearwaters and albatrosses. So killing it is in some sense taboo.'

Thus the mariner brings bad luck upon his shipmates. The wind drops, and the ship is becalmed for days on end, a scene so memorably evoked in the poem's best-known lines:

Water, water, everywhere,
And all the boards did shrink.
Water, water, everywhere,
Nor any drop to drink.

The blame passes squarely onto the shoulders of the eponymous mariner, for his act of casual destructiveness in killing the bird. As Mark Cocker notes: 'By slaying the albatross, the mariner brings disaster onto his crew, all of whom die except himself. And he is destined to travel throughout the rest of his life, repenting and telling the tale of his terrible destruction of this bird.'

Much has been written by literary critics about the possible meaning of *The Rime of the Ancient Mariner,* and we now know some of the background to the writing of the poem. Coleridge never saw an albatross himself – not even a stuffed specimen – and it seems that his fellow-poet William Wordsworth suggested the idea to him, when the two men were on a walk along the north Somerset coast.

According to a recent book by historian Robert Fowke, the poem is based on a true story, about an eighteenth-century sailor named Simon Hatley. It is said that in 1719, when rounding Cape Horn, the southernmost tip of South America, Hatley shot an albatross. The incident was reported by the captain of his ship, George Shelvocke, and almost eighty years later, at Wordsworth's suggestion, Coleridge read Shelvocke's account of the incident. As a result, he was inspired to write his famous poem.

Whatever the poem's origins, more than two centuries after it was first written, *The Rime of the Ancient Mariner* still evokes the needless nihilism that would characterise our relationship with seabirds, right up until the late nineteenth century.

*   *   *

Coleridge's mariner was a familiar figure during Britain's heyday as a maritime power, when the British Empire, 'on which the sun never set', covered more than one quarter of the world's landmass. At the height of this period in the nineteenth century, thousands of ships were travelling across the North Atlantic, bringing a wide range of goods and commodities back to Britain from the colonies. These mariners drove to extinction an extraordinary, flightless bird: the Great Auk – Britain's equivalent of the Dodo.

The Great Auk was, as its name suggests, the largest representative of the auk family. This is a group of about two dozen species of seabird found throughout the temperate and cooler regions of the northern hemisphere, and includes the familiar Puffin, Razorbill and Guillemot, as well as rarer and less well-known species such as the tiny auklets and murrelets of the Pacific Ocean.

The nearest thing we have to a Great Auk today is the Razorbill. But standing at 80 centimetres tall (against less than 40 centimetres for the Razorbill) the Great Auk would have dwarfed its smaller relative. Dark above, with white underparts, a white patch on its face and a huge, dagger-like bill, it must have been an impressive sight. For sailors travelling back and forth across the North Atlantic it would also have been a very familiar one, according to Rob Lambert: 'The Great Auk bred across the North Atlantic in an arc of islands from Newfoundland, through Iceland, Greenland and farther south to Orkney and Shetland. It was, perhaps at one stage, one of the commonest birds that have ever lived on the planet.'

Common it may have been, but the Great Auk had one major disadvantage over other seabirds: it was unable to fly. As a fish-eating seabird, with abundant prey and plenty of places to breed, it simply had no need to do so. Indeed the scientific name for the species, *Pinguinis impennis*, refers to the fact that the Great Auk was the original 'penguin'.

According to W. B. Lockwood, whose *Oxford Book of British Bird Names* is considered the leading work on the subject, the name 'penguin' was first coined in the late sixteenth century to describe the Great Auk, whose colonies had recently been discovered on the island of Newfoundland. By 1750 ornithologists were beginning to make a distinction between the 'northern penguin' (the Great Auk) and the 'southern penguin' – as we still call the family of flightless birds from the southern hemisphere. Only in 1768 – less than a century before the species went extinct – did Thomas Pennant coin the term 'Great Auk'.

For much of its existence, being flightless was not really a problem for the Great Auk. Terrestrial predators were unable to reach its nesting islands, and it was a strong swimmer, able to cover hundreds of miles across the surface of the sea. But as soon as the trade routes opened across the North Atlantic between Britain and her colonies in the New World, the Great Auk's days were numbered. Birder and broadcaster Tony Soper imagines the reaction of mariners on finding such a readily available supply of fresh meat: 'When the first whalers and fishermen went to the Davis Strait between Greenland and Newfoundland they were living on cod, of course, because that was what they were catching all day. And it must have been wonderful to be able to take a nice big fat juicy bird like a Great Auk.'

Near the British colony of Newfoundland, on the eastern seaboard of Canada, lay uninhabited seabird islands where Great Auks bred alongside their smaller relatives, Guillemots (known in North America as 'murres'), which still survive today. Because these islands were flat and accessible, very different from the steep seabird cliffs back home, these huge numbers of Great Auks were simply there for the taking. Jeremy Gaskell, author of a study of the bird's demise, *Who Killed the Great Auk?*, sets the scene:

It was perfectly possible to put a sail down, get your men ashore, get them to drive the birds onto the sail, tip them into the boat and have people on the boat just pluck them, then salt them; and that would keep you going for the rest of the time you were out at sea.

However many they killed, there were always masses of others.

Some ships simply drove the birds up a gangplank like human prisoners, and then kept them on the boat alive, killing them whenever they needed fresh meat.

Over time the Great Auk became even more valuable as a commodity, for its feathers, which were used to stuff pillows and bedding, as Jeremy Gaskell explains: 'The featherbed industry, in really quite a short space of time, caused such a huge destruction amongst these populations. Birds were just rounded up, driven into stone enclosures; then pulled out, clubbed, dunked into boiling water to get the feathers off quickly – and all this was being done on a huge, industrial scale.'

Perhaps the most grisly aspect of the auks' demise was that their bodies were so full of oil that this was used to fuel these fires – so the auks were boiled in a cauldron whose water was being heated by the oil from their erstwhile companions.

By the end of the eighteenth century, as a result of this wholesale killing, the Great Auk population was in a state of collapse on its main breeding grounds. So the birds were very rarely seen at the edge of their range, in places like St Kilda, and would no longer have been familiar to the islanders. David Attenborough describes events that took place there in 1840, just a few years before the Great Auk's span on Earth finally came to an end: 'There's a horrifying account of three men from St Kilda who went out to a small island, came round a corner and saw this huge bird – what turned out to be the last Great Auk in Britain.'

The men easily caught the bird, and kept it in captivity for a day or two. But then events took a sudden turn: the weather changed, and a storm blew up. The presumably terrified bird is said to have begun to make a shrieking noise. The equally terrified men became fearful, and decided that the bird must be a witch, and therefore was to blame for the storm – so they killed it.

Such was the demise of Britain's last Great Auk – the only British bird to go extinct in what ornithologists sometimes refer to as 'historical times' – defined as being since the year 1600. And yet Victorian bird experts could not accept that this was really happening to what had once been such an abundant species. Mark Cocker believes this is symptomatic of our perennial misunderstanding of the sea and its resources, which we mistakenly consider to be boundless and infinite: 'It is a measure of a kind of senseless abuse of the sea – it's the way in which we think the sea is limitless, and therefore we cannot believe that these resources are finite.'

But of course they are. We now know that the world's last Great Auk was killed on the island of Eldey, off the southern coast of Iceland, in June 1844. Even so, a decade later, two men still harboured the hope that a few individuals might have survived. Jeremy Gaskell begins their story: 'A couple of British ornithologists, John Wolley and his friend Alfred Newton, decided to make an expedition to Iceland to try to settle the question either way.' Wolley and Newton visited fishing communities and spoke to fishermen who remembered seeing Great Auks, and searched offshore islands for any evidence of the birds' presence. But all this effort was to no avail: they returned home empty-handed.

Later Alfred Newton wrote a valedictory article on the Great Auk for *The Ibis*, the prestigious journal of the British Ornithologists'

Union, in which he expressed the hope that some Great Auks might still survive, against all the odds. This caught the eye of the well-known Victorian novelist, the Reverend Charles Kingsley.

Newton's account provided the inspiration for a memorable scene in Kingsley's most famous book, *The Water-Babies*. The child hero, Tom, encounters the last Great Auk – or as it was also known, the garefowl: 'And there he saw the last of the gare-fowl, standing upon the All-Alone Stone, all alone.' Perched on a rocky outcrop, the elderly bird recounts the story of her species' demise: '"If you'd only had wings," said Tom, "then you might have all flown away too." '

Far from expressing sympathy or outrage at the extinction of this magnificent bird, Kingsley appears to be doing the exact opposite: his message being that creatures must evolve to suit the needs of a changing world, or face oblivion.

Today, in a more enlightened age, we find it hard to accept that such a magnificent creature should have vanished so easily, and with so little fanfare. In many ways the Great Auk was simply unlucky – had a few individuals managed to hang on in the remotest parts of its range, with today's knowledge and conservation methods we might have been able to save it for posterity. But once that last remaining individual had been killed it was, of course, lost forever.

*   *   *

Kingsley published *The Water-Babies* in 1863, in the midst of an unprecedented population explosion. During the course of the nineteenth century Britain's population almost quadrupled, rising from roughly 10.5 million in 1800 to more than 38 million in 1900. So to keep pace with demand for food, Britain's farmers needed to dramatically increase production on their land. Remarkably, it was seabirds that would fuel this agricultural revolution. Rural historian Jeremy Burchardt takes up the story: 'At this point, in the mid-nineteenth century, there was a fairly severe shortage of fertilisers – we just weren't keeping enough cattle to fertilise the land sufficiently just with their dung. So we needed to find other, alternative sources.'

Whoever came up with a solution to the fertiliser shortage was going to make a fortune. That man was a merchant called William Gibbs.

Gibbs sunk much of his vast wealth into the Tyntesfield estate, on the outskirts of Bristol, which he began building in 1863, creating what is undoubtedly one of the greatest architectural and cultural treasures of the Victorian age. But the source of Gibbs's fertile fortune was far less glamorous, according to a rhyme of the day:

Mr Gibbs made his tibbs,
Selling the turds of foreign birds...

For Tyntesfield – now owned by the National Trust – had very basic origins. It was built on a foundation of guano: the droppings of millions of seabirds. Mark Cocker believes that the tale of how this came about is one of the most shameful and inglorious episodes in the whole of Britain's long maritime history: 'Of all the stories of the abuse of a natural resource, guano is probably the most extreme.'

SEABIRDS

Although Britain's seven million seabirds produced plenty of guano, this was not the source that made Gibbs's fortune, as regular exposure to rain meant that many of the nutrients vital for its use as fertiliser simply leeched away. So instead, he collected guano from many thousands of miles away, on the edge of the Pacific Ocean off the coast of Peru.

Dr William Mathew, historian who has made a special study of the guano story, explains how a fortuitous combination of geographical, oceanographic and climatic factors led to the existence of these vast colonies of seabirds:

The particular feature of the coast of Peru was the Humboldt Current coming up from the south – a very cold current with upwellings of cold water. And this supported a huge plankton population; that then supported a huge fish population, in particular anchovies; and this fish population then supported an absolutely gigantic bird population. There were millions of birds on the one island at any particular time.

The main guano-producing birds were the Guanay Cormorant and the Brown Pelican. Over centuries, their droppings had accumulated to extraordinary depths; forming mineral-rich mountains. And because of the unusually dry climate, this particular source of guano was incredibly concentrated, according to William Mathew: 'Peruvian guano was widely recognised at the time as certainly the best fertiliser anywhere, because it was a natural product, and it had all the main plant foods: nitrogen, potash and phosphate.'

Using his undoubted entrepreneurial skills, William Gibbs had realised what an extraordinary profit might be made out of this unique source of fertiliser. He had begun importing guano in the 1840s, and later cleverly negotiated a deal with the Peruvian government, giving him a monopoly on the trade. But he still faced a problem – how to get the stuff back to Britain. As Jeremy Burchardt notes, he took an almighty risk in order to do so: 'In many respects it actually was quite an extraordinary thing to do. He was taking guano literally from the other side of the world; a very dangerous and difficult voyage around some of the stormiest seas in the world – around Cape Horn, and then right across the Atlantic.'

A dangerous and difficult voyage, certainly; but also a highly profitable one – especially when carried out on such a vast scale. Once the guano arrived in Britain, Gibbs sold it in huge quantities to farmers desperate for an efficient fertiliser, so that they could increase the productivity of their land, harvest more crops, and thereby feed the teeming millions in the fast-growing Victorian towns and cities. Guano gave a massive boost to the nation's agricultural output, so allowing the wheels of the Industrial Revolution to continue to turn. And it made William Gibbs the wealthiest commoner in England: the cost of building Tyntesfield – £70,000, somewhere between five and seven million pounds at today's values – was just one year's profits.

These untold riches were in stark contrast to the fate of the men actually mining the guano in Peru. The workforce was organised by Peruvian landowners, and relied on slaves, convicts and, by the 1850s, foreign indentured labour from thousands of miles away in Asia. Mark Cocker takes up the story: 'They took Chinese coolies, tying them into contracts they knew nothing about. They got to these desolate equatorial islands, and the conditions were completely appalling. Once the guano was loosened from the solid rock that it formed on the island, it became a noxious powder that blistered the lungs and nose.'

The plight of the foreign workers was exacerbated by their horrific workload – almost unimaginable by today's standards, as William Mathew has discovered: 'The normal amount a Chinese labourer would remove was five tons – sometimes eight tons – a day. And he had to do everything, from using a pickaxe to separate the manure from the stones; carrying the stuff to the edge of the cliffs, and dropping it down great canvas chutes into the boats below.'

Exhausted, far from home, and with no way of escaping what amounted to life as a slave, many workers chose to throw themselves off the cliffs to their death, rather than continue to suffer. They were simply replaced with another band of unfortunate souls.

Given the lack of regard for the human labourers, it is hardly surprising that there was no concern at all for the birds actually producing the guano. Their nest sites were destroyed by the mining, and wherever they went they were subject to continual disturbance. Unable to breed, they eventually disappeared from the islands. Mark Cocker sees this as symptomatic of the way we regard the sea and its seemingly boundless resources: 'It was typical of the boom-bust pattern of maritime harvests; it was one of the most grotesque dashes for growth, regardless of the consequences, there has ever been.'

The wanton destruction to man and bird in South America went largely unnoticed back in Britain. But by the 1860s – the very decade in which William Gibbs began to build his palatial residence – the welfare of seabirds at home could not be so easily ignored. For the first time voices were about to be raised against the unbridled exploitation of British seabirds.

* * *

The majority of Britain's seabird colonies are on remote, rocky, offshore islands, such as the Bass Rock, off the east coast of Scotland, and the Farne Islands, off Northumberland. The isolation of these places offers the birds some protection from terrestrial predators, both man and beast.

Nevertheless, there are a few seabird colonies on the British mainland, such as the cliffs of Bempton and Flamborough Head, in Yorkshire. These spectacular cliffs are a favourite haunt of the Kittiwake, one of the most delightful members of an often disregarded family, the gulls. Roy Dennis is just one of many birders who consider the Kittiwake to be one of their favourite seabirds: 'The Kittiwake is a very delicate gull, and also one which tells you its name! When you go to the colonies there it is, shrieking away, "kitt-i-waake, kitt-i-waake, kitt-i-waake..." It also has wings that look as if they have been dipped in black ink.'

But it was a difference in behaviour between the Kittiwake and other members of its family that made it peculiarly vulnerable, as Tim Birkhead explains:

The thing that makes the Kittiwake different from just about every other kind of gull is that it breeds on narrow cliff ledges, so is relatively safe from terrestrial predators. With birds like the Herring Gull or Black-headed Gull, if a predator like a fox or a hedgehog comes into the colony, all the birds fly up and mob that predator, and try to drive it away. Kittiwakes, on their narrow cliff ledges, never do that mobbing behaviour, because there's no value in it.

This tendency to sit tight made Kittiwakes very susceptible to human hunters. At Bempton and Flamborough Head local people had always harvested the seabirds for food – both their flesh and their eggs. A man would be lowered over the edge of the cliff on a rope, using a home-made harness. He would dangle in front of the ledges on the cliff face and fill his basket with the birds' eggs, before being pulled up by his companions.

By the Victorian period this had escalated into an intensive, commercial use of birds for meat, eggs and, in the case of Kittiwakes, their plumage. Mark Cocker describes the techniques used by the commercial bird-catchers: 'They would catch the birds, with nets, and they would cut the wings off – the parts they wanted – and then would throw the bird, wingless, back into the water.'

Just as with the plumage of many birds at this time, the feathers were then used by hatmakers in London, Paris and New York, to adorn their creations.

Those harvesting the birds in such a cruel and thoughtless way had no idea that they were in the wrong. As with all use and abuse of the animal kingdom, such behaviour was sanctioned and indeed legitimised by their Christian religious beliefs, as Rob Lambert notes: 'People who were harvesting the seabirds at Flamborough at that time were doing it for profit. But there was a sense of manifest destiny, that this was something that was given to them by bountiful Providence, and it was there to harvest and indeed that it would be wasteful not to.'

Harvesting the Kittiwakes for their feathers, though cruel, was at least commercially justifiable. But by the 1860s they became targets for a very different element of British society. This was the burgeoning middle classes – the *nouveaux riches* – who with greater wealth and free time were beginning to aspire to the leisure activities of the aristocracy. And these, of course, included the hunting, shooting and killing of wild birds.

Tim Birkhead points out the role played by the nineteenth-century transport revolution in fuelling this new sport: 'Once the railways made access to these coastal locations easier, hunting parties came to these seabird colonies to shoot these birds – which of course were so easy to shoot because they sat so tightly on their nests.'

After boarding so-called 'pleasure boats' in the harbour at Scarborough, groups of men would sail towards the colonies of birds. Once beneath the breeding cliffs, out would come the shotguns, and for hours on end they would simply shoot every bird within their sights. Mark Cocker describes the scene: 'They would blaze away at the parent birds sitting on eggs, killing as many as they could because the size of the bag was presumably the measure of the success of the "sport"; and this was having a devastating effect on breeding numbers.'

But the activities of these shooting parties didn't go unnoticed, according to Tim Birkhead: 'It was the sight of large numbers of dead and dying birds, and chicks whose parents had been killed with them left in the nest, that started to upset people.'

One person who took exception to this slaughter was the ornithologist Alfred Newton – the same man who, thirteen years earlier, had searched unsuccessfully for the last Great Auk. By then Newton had become a highly respected ornithologist. As the first Professor of Zoology at Cambridge University, and editor of the original ornithological journal *The Ibis*, he was a man of growing influence, whose opinions would be listened to.

Ever since his youth, when he and John Wolley had made that pointless journey to Iceland in search of the Great Auk, Newton had been acutely aware of the perils of extinction facing even the commonest birds, as Jeremy Gaskell notes: 'He had realised what had happened to the Great Auk a generation earlier; he saw that there was a chance of this happening again.'

So in 1868, to publicise his concerns about this wholesale slaughter of seabirds, Newton made a calculatedly emotional speech to the British Society for the Advancement of Science: 'At the present time I believe there is no class of animals so cruelly persecuted as the sea-fowl. That a stop should be put to this wanton and atrocious destruction of a species, I think none of my audience will deny.'

Just as he had hoped, his sensational speech was picked up by the press and widely reported. And for the first time, this touched a nerve with the British public, especially in the county where the killing of seabirds was taking place, as Rob Lambert explains: 'There was a sense developing that this slaughter on the cliffs was somehow to Yorkshire's shame, and a combination of local landowners, MPs and members of the clergy got together, and in 1868 formed an Association for the Protection of Seabirds.'

As a result of their work, a Bill for the Preservation of
Seabirds was presented to Parliament the following year. But as
Rob Lambert points out, the arguments they advanced to win
their case were very different from those that would be used in
any modern debate about bird protection. Instead of being based
on the intrinsic value of birds themselves, their aesthetic value or
concerns about cruelty, they focused almost exclusively on the
utilitarian value of these seabirds:

They came up with a fascinating strategy, based
on utilitarianism – this idea that the birds were
useful. They did two things: when the fishermen
of Bridlington were coming home on foggy days,
and they couldn't see the cliffs, the cries of the
seabirds alerted them to the presence of land.
The second argument was that the seabirds flew
inland and harvested pests on agricultural land.
And those two arguments carried the day.

The birds' fame grew so much that poems and ballads were written about them, and they were dubbed 'The Flamborough Pilots'
for their role in saving fishermen in peril. In June 1869 the
Seabirds Preservation Act finally came into law – the very first
Act of Parliament ever passed to protect British birds, and a full
twenty years before the founding of what would eventually
become the RSPB.

SEABIRDS

*   *   *

This marked a crucial turning point in the history of our relationship with seabirds. By the late Victorian era a new sensibility towards birds and other wildlife was beginning to emerge. We had finally begun to appreciate birds not just for how we could exploit them, but for their beauty, and for our delight in them.

And yet where seabirds were concerned, we still knew so little about their real lives, as Mark Cocker points out: 'One of the wonderful things about seabirds is that they are essentially very mysterious, and aspects of their behaviour are very little understood.'

This is almost as true today as it was during the early decades of the twentieth century. And although the mysteries about other groups of Britain's birds were gradually being investigated and solved, the lifecycle of seabirds would take much longer to unravel. At the forefront of these pioneering studies was a Welsh naturalist, Ronald Lockley.

Lockley was an extraordinary man: one of the great maverick ornithologists of the twentieth century, whose work had a huge influence on successive generations, even as his own status as one of our most important bird scientists began to fade.

In a writing career lasting well over sixty years, from 1930 to 1996, Lockley published more than fifty books. Many were evocative accounts of his beloved seabirds and the islands where they live, and they became firm favourites among a post-war public keen to share his escapist lifestyle. One of his best-known works, *The Private Life of the Rabbit*, was the inspiration for an even more famous book, Richard Adams's bestselling children's story *Watership Down.*

But as a young man Lockley hadn't set out to be a seabird scientist; in fact he was rather a dreamer, with an entrepreneurial streak. In the late 1920s, along with his first wife, he took a lease on an uninhabited island called Skokholm, off the south-west coast of Wales. His aim was to make money from fur, as historian of science Helen Macdonald explains: 'When Lockley turned up on Skokholm his initial plan was to make a lot of money; and he wanted to do this by breeding giant chinchilla rabbits, for their fur.'

Unfortunately, there was already an indigenous rabbit population on the island, eating the grass required by his chinchillas. So Lockley went to war, using all kinds of unpleasant means including cyanide gas, in order to eradicate them. But even before he could do so, external forces intervened, according to Helen Macdonald: 'His experiment failed completely because the market for rabbit skins for use in fashion completely crashed in the Great Depression.'

But Lockley's interest in seabirds was directly born out of this failure. While trying to trap the indigenous rabbits in their warrens he kept catching a strange, burrow-nesting bird instead – the Manx Shearwater.

The Manx Shearwater is a true seabird: a member of the order Procellariiformes – a large group of ocean-going birds including albatrosses and petrels as well as shearwaters. These birds are also known as 'tubenoses', because of the strange protrusion on top of their bill that enables them to locate food in the open ocean by smell.

But the Manx Shearwater is also something of a paradox. Although it is one of the least known of all Britain's birds, it is our most important species of seabird – at least 75 per cent of all the world's Manx Shearwaters breed in Britain and Ireland; somewhere between 300,000 and 370,000 pairs in all. Of these, almost 50,000 pairs breed on the island of Skokholm, where Lockley had made his island home.

The shearwaters would not have been immediately apparent to Lockley, partly because they spend the majority of the year at sea, only returning to Skokholm to breed, but mainly because of their nocturnal habits. Adults come back to their island breeding grounds under cover of darkness, to bring food for their hungry young. This is because, although their streamlined bodies and long, stiff wings are ideal for making long journeys across the world's oceans, they make the birds extremely vulnerable when they are on land. In sharp contrast to their effortless grace while flying over the sea, when they are on land shearwaters struggle to walk at all. If they returned by day, they would be easy pickings for the predatory Herring and Great Black-backed Gulls nesting on the island, which would catch them with ease.

So shearwaters return to their nests under cover of darkness, and call loudly to their young, in order to find the right burrow. The resulting noise has been known to confuse and terrify those hearing it for the first time – it sounds rather like a demented chicken crossed with an amusement arcade game. So when he first heard this strange cacophony, it took Lockley by surprise.

Until this time no one had attempted to study the habits of Manx Shearwaters, or indeed any other seabirds, in detail. Lockley soon became enthralled with these mysterious creatures, and devised imaginative – and increasingly ambitious – experiments to study the most intriguing aspects of their behaviour, as Mark Cocker reveals:

One of the things he was fascinated by was
the navigational capacity of Manx Shearwaters.
In one of these experiments he took a bird from
Skokholm to Devon, and released it – and within
a few hours the bird was back in its nest burrow.
Then he took this further and took a bird to
Venice. This was about a 900 kilometre [roughly
560 miles] journey over land, but of course a
seabird such as a Manx Shearwater would
almost certainly have taken a sea route,
which was a hugely circuitous one.

The bird's journey took it through the Mediterranean Sea to
Gibraltar, around the Iberian coast, across the Bay of Biscay and
English Channel, until it finally reached its native island of Skokholm
about seventeen days later – a journey of almost 4,000 kilometres
(2,800 miles). Mark Cocker is impressed – not only by Lockley's
obsession, but also by the bird itself: 'What this reveals is the
puniness of human travel efforts. This is a bird that has to find its
way across the open ocean, by itself, feeding and travelling for days.
I think this is what captivates us about seabirds in general – the
way they treat the open ocean, this featureless landscape, as home.'

Ronald Lockley wrote up his findings about the navigational
skills and breeding biology of his favourite bird in a book,
Shearwaters, published in 1942. But his ornithological legacy went
far beyond these amazing discoveries. On Skokholm he had also
created Britain's very first bird observatory, in 1933. This

pioneering institution for the study of migrating land and sea birds started off a nationwide boom in migration studies, which flourished in the years following the Second World War. Its legacy can still be seen today, in the thriving network of bird observatories on islands and coastal headlands up and down the country.

But for Lockley himself the war brought about exile from his beloved island. Skokholm was commandeered by the armed forces, and he moved across the water to mainland Pembrokeshire, where he spent his time farming and working in conservation, as well as continuing his prolific writing career. Disillusioned with what he regarded as the British government's poor attitude towards conservation, Ronald Lockley spent his later years living in another seabird haven, New Zealand, before his death in 2000 at the age of ninety-six.

*   *   *

From early on in the Second World War, the German sea blockade of Britain had resulted in severe food shortages. So, despite bird protection laws, seabirds were back on the menu, for the first time in a generation. Roy Dennis, who in the 1960s was warden of the bird observatory on Fair Isle, between Orkney and Shetland, recalls islanders telling him about the wartime seabird harvest:

Shags were eaten in the war, as were Cormorants; in fact most birds would have been eaten in wartime. They shot Shags on Fair Isle, and sent them to London for food; but instead

of calling them Shags they called them 'black
ducks'. So by the end of the war Shags
were very scarce, and as soon as they
saw a boat they were in flight!

But this use of seabirds for meat was short-lived, driven purely
by necessity. In the post-war period our contact with ocean-
going seabirds would begin to diminish. Gradually Britain's
maritime power also waned and, along with the decline in deep-
sea fishing, this meant that fewer and fewer people made their
living at sea.

The decades following the end of the Second World War
also saw the demystification of some of our commonest seabirds,
gulls. This was largely thanks to a refugee scientist from the
Netherlands named Niko Tinbergen, who arrived in Britain to work
at Oxford University shortly after the end of the conflict. Helen
Macdonald explains the crucial importance of Tinbergen's work:

Tinbergen was one of the great pioneers
of animal behaviour studies in the field. He saw
that the kind of experiments that had been
going on, which involved looking at animals in
cages, in captivity, were pretty pointless; because
he thought that animals in captivity wouldn't
display the kind of behaviours they would in
the wild. So what he did was to take animal
behaviour studies out into the field – a very
groundbreaking thing to have done.

SEABIRDS

Born in 1907, Tinbergen grew up in the Netherlands and, as a teenager, became interested in nature study. But, when he was in his early thirties, his promising career as a zoologist was rudely interrupted by the Nazi occupation of his homeland. He was even imprisoned in a concentration camp for his political views, after taking a firm and principled stand against the internment of his Jewish colleagues at the University of Leiden.

This experience was to shape both his later research and the way he carried out his work, according to zoologist, author and broadcaster Desmond Morris, who studied animal behaviour under Tinbergen at Oxford University, and came to know him well: 'Having been kept in prison left his mark on him, because he was so passionate about getting away from his Oxford laboratories and getting out into the field.'

At Oxford – and for much of the time away from it – Tinbergen pioneered a revolutionary new method of intensive field study. He chose gulls as his main subject, partly because they displayed a suite of fascinating behaviours, but also because they were so common and widespread, as Desmond Morris recalls: 'One of Niko's principles in studying birds was to always go for the most common species. The more common and populous a bird is, the easier it is to study. And so he loved gulls!'

Tinbergen's research on gulls was popularised through a book in the Collins New Naturalist series, *The Herring Gull's World*, which was published in 1953 and remained in print as a core university textbook until the 1980s. In the late 1960s, he also presented a prize-winning TV film, *Signals for Survival*, made with broadcaster Hugh Falkus for the BBC. Helen Macdonald finds Tinbergen's presentational style both entertaining and highly revealing: 'The beginning of the film is great – he starts off by shaking his fist at the camera and scowling, to show that there are signals for aggression which everyone understands.'

Helen Macdonald also believes that the film gives voice to Tinbergen's own anxieties about the nature of aggression in humans, a legacy of his traumatic wartime experiences: 'It's about a gull colony, and how gull colonies are always just at the edge of chaos and aggression. There are chicks being eaten by the other adult gulls, and it's a complete disaster zone in all sorts of ways.'

Hugh Falkus's narration to the film confirms this viewpoint: 'This is a great bird city; this is a city of thieves and murderers; they are all potential killers and eaters of their neighbours' chicks. But social life in bird city is made possible by a highly complex system of communication – a language comprising posture, movement, colour and sound.'

The film shows that the gulls had evolved a complex system of very precise patterns of behaviour and signals to one another. Because every gull knows and understands these codes of behaviour, this keeps the colony from tipping over the edge into complete chaos, according to Helen Macdonald:

If you look at the way in which this is presented in the programme, it's very clear that Tinbergen himself was very worried about the way that humans were going, and he thought that in the future, with overpopulation and crowding, it was all going to be disastrous. So

he saw this as a kind of lesson for humanity –
how to negotiate these primal instincts.

Through his books and television appearances, Tinbergen's work reached an audience far beyond the narrow academic world in which he had started his work on gulls. In 1973, he shared the Nobel Prize with two Austrian biologists, Karl von Frisch and Konrad Lorenz (who, ironically, had been accused of collaboration with the Nazi regime during the war), for their work on individual and social behaviour patterns in animals. He died at his home in Oxford in 1988, aged eighty-one.

Tinbergen's legacy was enormous, and owed a vast amount to his meticulous and insightful studies of seabirds. During his lifetime the way we thought about the natural world changed beyond recognition; a change seen in his work, which managed both to reflect many of the wider ecological anxieties of the era, as well as revealing the habits of seabirds to the viewing public.

And yet, as we became a nation of landlubbers, seabirds generally became even more remote from our daily lives. They were increasingly out of sight and out of mind. But then, literally overnight, on 18 March 1967, one event would change all this forever.

*   *   *

According to Rob Lambert, 'If there was one moment in our history when seabirds truly invaded our national consciousness, it was the *Torrey Canyon* disaster.' Rob Lambert has made a special study of the *Torrey Canyon* and, when you look at the facts, it's hard to disagree with him. As the nation awoke to breakfast on the morning of Saturday 18 March 1967, and looked at the front pages of their newspapers or turned on the BBC Home Service, they were faced with an environmental catastrophe unprecedented in living memory.

The *Torrey Canyon*, the world's thirteenth-largest supertanker, had been chartered by British Petroleum (BP), to bring a cargo from Kuwait to the port of Milford Haven in South Wales. It had run aground on the Seven Stones Reef, a treacherous series of undersea rocks lying to the west of Land's End, and to the northeast of the Isles of Scilly, off the coast of Cornwall. On board was a phenomenal 120,000 tonnes of crude oil – and now much of this was fast leaking into the sea, creating an oil slick at least eight miles long, which was growing by the hour.

As Rob Lambert points out, this was an eminently avoidable disaster, entirely the product of human error – the misjudgement, indeed, of just one man, the ship's captain:

On the evening of Friday, 17 March, the *Torrey Canyon* was rushing to catch the tide at Milford Haven, and the ship's captain decided – against all established thinking, which was to go round to the west of the Isles of Scilly, and then swing round into the Bristol Channel – instead to cut through the gap between the Scillies and Land's End. Overnight he managed to run aground this enormous ship on the Seven Stones Reef.

The *Torrey Canyon* was the first environmental disaster to unfold in the television era, meaning that it became far better known than previous such events. But what gave it even more impact, according to Rob Lambert, was the effect the oil was having on the natural world:

Perhaps the most powerful images of the *Torrey Canyon* disaster were not what we might have expected. It was not the broken ship lying on the Seven Stones Reef – the most powerful images were of seabirds covered in oil being washed up on the Cornish beaches. These were pitiful images, which said an awful lot to us about our mastery of, and domination over, the natural world. They certainly were emotive, and people reacted to them. Seabird centres all over Cornwall were inundated with boxload after boxload of seabirds – all sadly doomed to die.

One man on the frontline was Tony Soper, a young broadcaster and naturalist, who reported on the disaster for the local BBC news:

We had no idea how much damage this was likely to cause, but in West Cornwall they had a big problem with Guillemots, Razorbills, Shags and so on. Any number of outfits were trying to clean the birds up – people were setting up rescue stations right, left and centre; especially in hairdressing salons, because they had the little showers for doing people's hair. And they were putting detergent on these birds, which of course got the oil off very effectively, but left them without any grease and they couldn't fly. So an awful lot of birds were put back in the sea totally unable to manage.

A disaster on this scale required decisive action from the government, and the Prime Minister, Harold Wilson, soon waded in. Wilson already had a special interest in this part of the world, as Rob Lambert points out: 'He of course was viewing this not only as our national leader, but also as somebody who was intimately involved with the Isles of Scilly. He had holidayed there since the 1950s, and it was his own personal paradise.'

In an effort to spare the beaches and the seabird colonies from the oil, and also to be seen to be doing something decisive, Wilson's government made the controversial – and as it turned out – misguided decision to bomb the stricken vessel. So the Fleet Air Arm sent Blackburn Buccaneer aircraft, from Lossiemouth in Scotland, to drop tonnes of bombs, and even napalm, in an attempt to ignite the fuel in the hull, in the hope that it would all burn off. Wilson himself stood on the top of the island of St Martin's with the people of Scilly, to watch as the bombs were dropped.

But even after the ship was sunk, a large quantity of oil made its way to the shore, and a massive clean-up effort was required. Tony Soper recalls what happened next: 'BP poured masses of detergent all the way along the beaches in order to disperse the oil, which in the long run we realised was a mistake.'

In the aftermath of the disaster the nation reflected on how ill-prepared it had been for such an environmental catastrophe, as Rob Lambert notes: 'There was a powerful realisation in government that there was no overarching administrative body to deal with an environmental disaster like this in Britain.'

Today, the wreck of the *Torrey Canyon* lies out of view, some thirty metres beneath the surface of the sea. But its influence on environmental policy can still be felt. Following the disaster, the Royal Commission on Pollution led to important changes in government, including the first ever Department for the Environment to be set up anywhere in the world. Future oil spills, including the *Braer* on Shetland in 1993, and the *Sea Empress* off the coast of Pembrokeshire in 1996, would be dealt with much more rapidly and efficiently, thanks to the painful lessons learned from the *Torrey Canyon* disaster.

*   *   *

For a few weeks in early 1967, environmental disaster had propelled seabirds into our national consciousness. It also made us realise how little we actually knew about these mysterious birds. Tim Birkhead has spent much of his life studying seabirds, and points out that at the time our understanding of seabirds was severely hampered by a lack of concrete information about their numbers and distribution.

So, soon afterwards, helped partly by funding from the *Torrey Canyon* Appeal Fund, scientists launched the first ever nationwide seabird census to take stock of our breeding colonies. Named 'Operation Seafarer', after an ancient Anglo-Saxon poem featuring seabirds written more than thirteen centuries earlier, the survey used more than 1,000 volunteers to survey every single site for breeding seabirds around the coasts of Britain and Ireland. The results of the census, which took place in 1969 and 1970, were published in book form in 1973, and have since served as a valuable baseline for subsequent research on rises and declines in our seabird populations.

But seabirds might easily have slipped from public view once again, were it not for a dramatic change in the behaviour of one particular group: gulls. For better or worse, this change would bring more of us into direct contact with seabirds than ever before.

'Seagulls', as we often call them, are undoubtedly the most familiar of all Britain's seabirds. From childhood holidays at the seaside, to the theme music for *Desert Island Discs*, the evocative cry of the Herring Gull is etched on the consciousness of a whole nation.

Until recently this large, noisy gull was hardly ever seen away from the coast – indeed a commonly held belief was that the arrival of gulls inland was a sure sign of a storm out at sea. But things have rapidly changed for this familiar species, and author and birder Jeremy Mynott believes he knows why: 'The poor old Herring Gull – well, there's no Herring Gull that's seen a herring for the last fifty years! They live on other things now.'

The need to find alternative sources of food has brought them starkly into view in our everyday lives, as Christopher Frayling points out:

Most people encounter seabirds
today because of some shock-horror story
about gulls eating the flake from your 'Mister
Softee' ice-cream in a city centre! They're not
exotic, they're not 'the other' any more – and
they're a problem when they get out of their
own sphere. Our attitude is 'Keep to the
ocean, but don't invade my territory!'

Two main species have moved inland: the Lesser Black-backed
Gull, and its larger and paler-winged relative, the Herring Gull.
They now commonly nest in a growing number of city centres,
including Cardiff, Birmingham, Bristol and London. Birder and
writer David Lindo, who lives and works in London, encounters
these birds virtually every day: 'They're obvious birds, they're
big birds, and they're going about their business in a very obvious way, so we're seeing all aspects of their lives: we're seeing
their courtship, nesting, laying eggs and feeding their young.'

It is when the gulls are raising a family that natural biological behaviour rears its head – and as David Lindo points out,
that's something we find hard to deal with: 'During that process
they become quite aggressive, and that's a shock to us, because in
our little lives in cities we don't expect that sort of behaviour.
That doesn't happen here – it happens out in the country or on
television, but not in my city!'

And encounters with these large, feisty birds can be very
memorable. When he was a young seabird researcher, Tim
Birkhead had first-hand experience of a gull attack: 'This gull

came down making this terrible wheezing noise which I can still remember, put both feet out, and hit me on the back of the head.'

That sounds bad enough – but things then got a whole lot worse: 'It then vomited and defecated simultaneously, so I got vomit down the front of my head and gull shit down my neck, and it left me feeling sick all day long – not because of the defecation but because the whack on the back of my head was so unexpected!'

Our contemporary dislike for gulls in our towns and cities is in stark contrast to the way we used to feel about them when they lived at the coast. Perhaps it is part of our tendency to dislike creatures that, like us, are adaptable and successful. Yet ironically, it was our own efforts to solve a major pollution problem that, quite inadvertently, created the conditions that would encourage gulls to settle inland.

The Great Smog of December 1952 was the worst air pollution event in Britain's history. It is thought to have killed somewhere between 4,000 and 12,000 people, mainly the elderly and very young. Another 100,000 people were made ill with respiratory diseases.

The government's response to this devastating event was the 1956 Clean Air Act, which prevented the burning of household waste in home fireplaces. As well as producing an increase in the amount of waste that would previously have been burned, this also coincided with the start of an unprecedented consumer boom from the late 1950s onwards. This, in turn, led to a further large increase in the amount of domestic waste being produced.

So, in the following decades, ever-increasing quantities of rubbish were hauled off to landfill sites, providing a bonanza for the gulls. Tens of thousands of them moved inland, to take advantage of these easy pickings; and having found plenty of food, they also found the perfect places to nest nearby, on our city roofs. Here they are safe from ground predators such as rats and foxes, in what ecologists describe as an 'analogue habitat' to their natural home. David Lindo believes that this invasion of our space is not the gulls' fault, but our own: 'They are victims of our excess.'

Gulls are the most adaptable of all seabirds, with extraordinarily catholic tastes, but their scavenging behaviour does not always endear them to us, as Jeremy Mynott notes: 'The gulls are exploiting as a food supply human waste, about which we ourselves feel some disgust. They became in some sense a metaphor for this waste, and I think that's part of why they have attracted so much hostility.'

Gull populations in some British cities have now grown to the point where they are considered vermin. And yet, especially if we live in these cities, we are only aware of part of the picture, according to Mark Cocker: 'We have a sense of gulls being ubiquitous and commonplace, but in fact one of the most frequent nesters on people's roofs – the Herring Gull – has declined substantially. Half of all Herring Gulls have gone in about the last fifty years.'

In 2009 this familiar bird was added to the Red List of Birds of Conservation Concern in the UK. Just like two other members of this unfortunate club, the Starling and the House Sparrow, it seems hard to believe that such an apparently common and ubi-quitous bird should have declined so precipitously, in such a short period of time.

The reason for the fall in numbers is because the original coastal colonies of Herring Gulls have collapsed, due to a lack of food. Fishermen no longer lay out their catches on the harbour side, nor gut fish at sea. Over-fishing has also reduced the birds' food supply. Herring Gulls have survived until now because they are truly exceptional – they have managed to adapt, in a very short time, from living by the sea to their new urban homes. But other species may not be so lucky, as Roy Dennis, who has spent a lifetime studying seabirds, points out: 'We are not managing the marine resources in Britain and Europe well, and the seabirds show us that.'

*   *   *

Sadly for us, our best-loved seabird, the Puffin, is one of the species now in decline. Even though most of us have never seen a Puffin, we feel we know this comical little bird, the model for countless children's toys, and the inspiration for the world's most celebrated series of children's books. Like many birders, Tony Soper has a soft spot for this characterful little bird: 'It's like a toy animal, really – you just look at it, and you simply cannot believe that this is the real thing! It cannot be a real bird – how can it exist like that?!'

We used to exploit Puffins just as we did other seabirds – for food, fuel and feathers – but in recent years they have moved into a central place in our affections. So it is ironic, at a time when we have finally come to appreciate them, that we may now be threatening their existence.

The Puffin's predicament provides a salutary warning for the future of our relationship with seabirds, and ironically our classic image of the species is a signal of its plight, as Roy Dennis explains: 'The iconic view of a Puffin is this bird with this incredibly bright bill, coming ashore and running up to its burrow with all these little fish arranged in its bill, head to tail.'

SEABIRDS

Puffins feed these nutritious little fish, sand eels, to their growing chicks. In recent years many chicks have starved to death because of a shortage of sand eels. This is partly due to over-fishing, but it is also the result of the even more serious long-term problem of global climate change. As marine temperatures increase at a more rapid rate than those on land, the very nature of the seas where Puffins search for food is changing. Seabird enthusiast and RSPB President Kate Humble explains the problem: 'Sea temperatures are rising, and this means that species of fish such as sand eels that support our seabirds are heading north into cooler waters. And what's going to follow them? Our seabirds.'

In the last ten years, the reduction in food supply brought about by climate change has already contributed to a significant fall in the total number of seabirds breeding in Britain. If this continues, Kate Humble believes that it will have repercussions far beyond purely biological and ecological ones; it will affect our nation's cultural life too: 'If we lost our seabirds, we would not just be losing colonies of birds – we would be losing a part of our heritage, a part of what makes Britain Britain.'

Arguably, we have lost much of this heritage already. As our dependence on seabirds gradually diminished, we developed a deeper aesthetic appreciation of them. But at the same time, their cultural relevance to us began to recede – in the modern world, they are simply less central to our lives than birds we encounter every day in our gardens or the wider countryside. We may have protected seabirds, and learned more about them, but now our mismanagement of the seas threatens their very future.

So today, they float in our peripheral vision, as ghostly reminders of the seafaring people we once were.

COUNTRYSIDE
BIRDS

The birds of Britain's countryside are among the most familiar and iconic of all our birds. For centuries, we've celebrated them in music and poetry, used them to forecast changes in the weather and the seasons, and hunted them for food and sport.

Throughout our long history, these birds have not just shaped the appearance of the British countryside – but also defined its very nature, according to author and ornithologist Jeremy Mynott: 'The countryside birds, in my view, are a constitutive part of the countryside: you can't describe the countryside without describing the birds.'

This is the story of the deep, age-old connection between the birds of the British countryside and the people of these islands. It tells of how we have used and abused them, celebrated them and cherished them, and watched their fortunes rise – and fall. And how, at the eleventh hour, we have finally come to understand what they – and the countryside – really mean to us.

*   *   *

Wherever you look in the British countryside, at whatever the time of year – spring, summer, autumn or winter – you will find birds. Farmland birds, such as the Skylark, Grey Partridge, Lapwing and Yellowhammer, have lived alongside us for more than ten thousand years, ever since our ancestors first cleared the forests that covered much of Britain, to prepare the land for agriculture.

So it is hardly surprising that, when they needed to mark the changing of the seasons, our forebears turned to these familiar creatures. And although we have lost many of our age-old connections with nature and the countryside, the use of birds as seasonal markers has survived into the twenty-first century, as Jeremy Mynott notes: 'Birds are very important seasonal markers in Britain – and not just for birdwatchers, but for ordinary people too. Everybody – or at least everybody of a certain age – still thinks of the first Swallow, and the first Cuckoo, as a way of marking the change of the season.'

For Andrew Motion, this annual habit of using natural events to mark the coming of spring has a profound connection with what makes us human beings:

You would have to be very dull of soul indeed not to be moved by the life of the Swallow, for instance. The Swallow has a very important part in our national idea of what it is like to be British: we time our seasons by its coming and going, in an absolutely primitive and very ancient kind of way – it's in our bones.

The coming of the Swallow each spring is also a key event in the life of ornithologist and broadcaster Tony Soper: 'The way Swallows come and whistle and sing is a very joyous arrival; and the fact that it makes its home in your outbuildings – your shed or garage if you leave the door open – is something that you really seriously look forward to each year.'

The Swallow, by virtue of being common and widespread, is the main species we associate with the coming of spring, at least in rural Britain. But the change in the season has also long been marked by the annual appearance of a letter in *The Times* newspaper, commenting on the arrival of another visitor to our shores: the Cuckoo. Indeed a collection of letters to that august newspaper, entitled *The First Cuckoo*, contained several items of correspondence signalling the return of this iconic bird. These included the following letter, written on 6 February 1913, by Mr R. Lydekker from Hertfordshire:

> Sir,
> While gardening this afternoon, I heard a faint note, which
> led me to say to my under-gardener, who was working
> with me, 'Was that the Cuckoo?' Almost immediately
> afterwards we both heard the full double note of a cuckoo,
> repeated either two or three times... There is not the
> slightest doubt that the song was that of a cuckoo.

Unfortunately for this particular correspondent, it turned out that there was indeed cause for doubt, as he shamefacedly revealed in another letter published six days later:

Sir,
I regret to say that… I have been completely deceived
in the matter of the supposed cuckoo. The note was
uttered by a bricklayer's labourer at work on a house in
the neighbourhood of the spot whence the note appeared
to come…

Mr Lydekker may have been the victim of a cruel and embarrassing hoax, but later generations have continued to mark and celebrate the Cuckoo's annual return. Broadcaster Kate Humble recalls the importance of the bird during her childhood in the Chilterns: 'We always used to talk about hearing the first Cuckoo, and my parents would always say, "Should we write to *The Times*? Oh no, someone got there a week before us…" And it was this lovely tradition.'

It is a tradition that goes back many centuries – one of the very first poems written in something close to modern English, probably written during the middle part of the thirteenth century, features as its central motif the Cuckoo's return:

Sumer is icumen in,
Lhude sing cuccu!

Local communities all over Britain – and indeed farther afield in Europe – would mark the bird's appearance, with key dates in the calendar being associated with its remarkably regular date of arrival.

So in Sussex the bird is due on 14 April, in Cheshire 15 April, Worcestershire 20 April and Yorkshire 21 April – dates often celebrated by the holding of an annual 'Cuckoo Fair', where villagers and townspeople would welcome the bird's return back to their neighbourhood – the ideal excuse, perhaps, for a spring festival. Cuckoos were also associated with other signs of spring – the common wetland flower lady's smock is also known as 'cuckoo-flower', because it bloomed at the same time as the bird's arrival; while 'cuckoo-pint' (the arum lily, also known as 'Lords and Ladies') and 'cuckoo-spit' (the strange, frothy home of the froghopper larva) also get their name from this bird.

The Cuckoo has given rise to a number of local rhymes, most of which are variations on the same theme – the brevity of the bird's time with us, and the changes we notice during its stay:

In April I open my bill;
In May I sing all day;
In June I change my tune;
In July away I fly;
In August away I must.

All these varied ways of marking the return of one migrant bird reveal just how ingrained the Cuckoo has become in our culture. But this very British ritual may now be coming to an end. The Cuckoo is suffering a catastrophic decline – because of food shortages in Britain, and drought in Africa, where it spends the winter.

In the first British Trust for Ornithology Atlas survey, carried out from 1968–72, the Cuckoo was found in roughly 90 per cent of ten-kilometre squares in Great Britain. Since then its decline has been precipitous, with bird numbers falling by more than 50 per cent in England and Wales, though oddly Scottish

Cuckoos appear to be holding their own. In 2009, journalist Mike McCarthy drew the bird's plight to the attention of the wider public in his book, *Say Goodbye to the Cuckoo*. This prompted many ordinary people to realise that they no longer heard the call of the Cuckoo, in places where it had once been common.

The Cuckoo's decline threatens not just the bird itself, but its cultural status too, as environmentalist Chris Baines points out: 'There's a whole folk culture across the northern hemisphere about the Cuckoo. If you have to explain what the Cuckoo was, you've kind of lost the point of that cultural aspect to birds.'

Ornithologist and writer Mark Cocker agrees:

It's the way in which a bird like the Cuckoo can move from being the birthright of every rural inhabitant of the British Isles – even though Cuckoos were never especially numerous, they make such a distinctive sound, they're so ubiquitous, and so adapted to all sorts of environments – but there are now large swathes of the UK where Cuckoos are never heard, and may never be heard again.

The fate of the Cuckoo has been mirrored in the fortunes of many other birds of the British countryside. Familiar species such as the Skylark, Grey Partridge, Lapwing and Yellowhammer – along with less well-known ones such as the Tree Sparrow and

Corn Bunting – have all suffered major declines in recent years, falling victim to the seemingly unstoppable industrialisation of our farmed landscape. All too often our short-term interests, such as the desire for ever cheaper food, have taken precedence over theirs, to the continued detriment of their fortunes.

*   *   *

The current status of our rural birds may be a cause for concern. But not so very long ago, towards the end of the eighteenth century, the British countryside and its birds were still living together in a state of comparative harmony. We know this through the life and writings of one remarkable man – the Reverend Gilbert White, author of *The Natural History of Selborne*.

Since it first appeared, in 1789, this modest little book has never been out of print – an amazing achievement, as Jeremy Mynott points out: 'Gilbert White is an extraordinary phenomenon. He is said to be the fourth most published author in the English language – and this is quite extraordinary for a country vicar writing what was in effect a series of nature notes.'

Even today, White's writings feel as fresh and insightful as on the day they were first published. Take this observation of the mating habits of our most aerial bird, the Swift: 'The swift is almost continually on the wing; and as it never settles on the ground, on trees, or roofs, would seldom find opportunity for amorous rites, was it not enabled to indulge them in the air.'

More than two centuries after this was written, broadcaster David Attenborough continues to be enthralled and amazed by White's skills of observation: 'He was remarkable – after all, without binoculars, he saw the mating of the Swift, up in the sky... I'm sure I couldn't possibly have noticed that.'

But White wasn't just a good observer – he was also an excellent and perceptive naturalist, at a time when many things we now take for granted about Britain's birds had yet to be discovered.

For example, he was the first person to realise that three different kinds of small green warbler visit Britain each spring and summer. Despite having no optical aids such as binoculars to help him, he successfully differentiated the Chiffchaff, Willow Warbler and Wood Warbler from one another, whereas previous writers had assumed there was just a single species. He did so not simply by looking at the birds, but by listening to them too, thereby discovering that their three songs were quite different: 'I have now, past dispute, made out three distinct species of the willow-wren, which constantly and invariably use distinct notes.'

Even today, despite the huge advances in the optical quality of binoculars since White's day, modern birders still often use these three species' different songs to tell them apart.

White's enduring appeal may also be because he concentrates almost entirely on his own quiet little corner of the English countryside – the rural parish of Selborne, in Hampshire – as Jeremy Mynott explains: 'He was born and died in the village which he describes, and you get the sense that he knows it so intimately that he would know if a bird arrived or a leaf fell overnight.'

As a lecturer in rural history, Jeremy Burchardt has also noted the importance of White's local roots: 'What is quite remarkable about Gilbert White's work is the sense that it is a kind of microcosm of English country life. It's as if, in a way, you can find the whole of nature within the manageable confines of one English village.'

Mark Cocker who, as one of the contributors to the *Guardian*'s Country Diary, celebrates the wildlife of his own Norfolk parish, sees this precise localism as the key aspect to understanding the enduring appeal of White's writings: 'He redeemed the word "parochial" from its sense of narrowness and limitation; he exalts the parish as a place where all life exists, and we can follow in his footsteps.'

Today, it may seem surprising that Gilbert White's diary of natural events should have become so popular, and indeed remained so. Perhaps this is because it portrays a very comforting image of the countryside: a tranquil, unchanging landscape, filled with the sound of birds. Just like another writer from our rural past, much of this appeal may be pure nostalgia. Although she was writing a few decades after White, Jane Austen shares his ability to focus on one small corner of the world, and yet at the same time draw lessons on a much wider scale. Both White and Austen lived in the same county – indeed her home in Chawton is only a few miles away from Selborne – and both have developed a reputation as chroniclers of a rural way of life now long since lost to us. It's an attraction that grows ever more potent as the years pass, as David Attenborough points out: "Why do we look at all these charming ladies in bonnets on our television sets? It's a picture of rural, eighteenth-century England which we find charming.'

Yet for all the undoubted charm contained within the pages of *The Natural History of Selborne*, and for all its continued fascination to modern naturalists today, cultural historian Christopher Frayling takes a slightly more sceptical view. He believes that in his obsession with one small corner of England, its author may have been hiding his fears about changes afoot in the wider world:

There's Gilbert White, sitting in his parsonage, looking at what's going on in his back garden and in the fields beyond. And then you say to yourself, 'It was published in 1789 – and what happened then?' The French Revolution is happening on the continent; the Industrial Revolution is happening in England; massive social change, but no reference to the real world that's going on beside him? And that kind of obsessiveness sometimes worries me – it's wonderful, but there's a slight feeling of 'Stop the world – I want to get off'.

*   *   *

During Gilbert White's lifetime, some things didn't change. The birds of Britain's countryside continued to thrive alongside us, as we farmed the land in the age-old, traditional ways.

But in the decades following his death in 1793, the little world he documented so carefully would be turned upside down. The countryside would be transformed forever as a result of a major and unprecedented agricultural revolution, and the birds that lived there would begin a long period of decline, from which many have yet to recover.

One bird, more than any other, symbolises the loss of this traditional landscape. It is a bizarre, shy and elusive relative of the Coot: the Corncrake. About the size and shape of a Moorhen, the Corncrake is a buffish-brown colour, with mottled upper-parts, streaked flanks and a short, stubby bill. But because it is so seldom seen, it is the Corncrake's call – a pair of grated notes, constantly repeated for hours on end – which has earned it fame. The sound is even embodied in the bird's scientific name: *Crex crex*.

As a lifelong birder, Bill Oddie has had his fair share of frus-trating encounters with this mysterious creature:

I remember the first one I heard, many years ago on Shetland, I didn't realise what I was listening to for a while, and then I finally thought, 'Aah! It's a Corncrake!' Then, your problems begin, because they can throw their voice. So you think it's just over there, and you go just over there, but it isn't – and yet it's still calling; so you end up going round and round and round this little field, and you still can't see it!

At the start of the nineteenth century, the strange, repetitive call of the Corncrake was a familiar sound of spring and summer throughout the British countryside, all the way from Scilly to Shetland. For one of Gilbert White's disciples, the poet and naturalist John Clare, the Corncrake – or as he called it, the landrail – was the classic sound of summer:

How sweet and pleasant grows the way
Through summer time again
While Landrails call from day to day
Amid the grass and grain

We hear it in the weeding time
When knee deep waves the corn
We hear it in the summers prime
Through meadows night and morn…

John Clare, the Northamptonshire farm labourer who found fame as a poet, was also a brilliant self-taught naturalist. Born in 1793, just seventeen days after White had died, he spent his early years in the village of Helpston, on the western edge of what remained of the East Anglian Fens.

Originally celebrated and patronised, and later dismissed, by the literary world as the 'peasant poet', Clare's reputation was salvaged from the mid-twentieth century onwards. Ornithologist James Fisher, one of his early champions, memorably described him as 'the finest poet of Britain's minor naturalists, and the finest naturalist of Britain's major poets.'

Clare was certainly an excellent and perceptive observer of birds – especially given that, like Gilbert White, he had no binoculars or telescope to help him identify them. Clare identified at least 120, and probably nearer 150, different species of bird in and around his home village. These included rare visitors such as the Osprey, and even a convincing description of what appears to have been a juvenile Greater Flamingo, a species that is still not on the official British List.

But it was Clare's observations and writings on the more familiar birds of the British countryside that set him apart from anyone else. More than any other writer, before or since, he celebrated these birds and their daily lives in forensic detail. Spare his style may be, but in a few words he can evoke a sense of place, or the essence of a bird, better than anyone, as in the opening lines of his sonnet 'Emmonsailes Heath in Winter':

> I love to see the old heath's withered brake
> Mingle its crimpled leaves with furze and ling
> While the old heron from the lonely lake
> Starts slow and flaps his melancholy wing...

Like many poets before him, Andrew Motion is struck by the highly specific nature of Clare's prose and poetry:

In the minuteness of his attention, in his faithfulness to things as they actually are, he is the best writer about birds there has ever been in the English language. What he has, to a greater degree than anyone else, is an eye for detail, and relish for the ordinary; which means that the ordinary is always being turned into the miraculous. So when we read the poems we really do feel it's like standing in a wood and

listening to a Nightingale, or walking through
a field and seeing a Corncrake.

Jeremy Burchardt also contrasts Clare's simple style with his
better-known poetic contemporaries such as Byron, Keats and
Shelley, who favoured far more ornate language and imagery:
'Rather than speaking in grand, rhetorical terms, as many of the
great Romantic poets did, he is really closely attentive to the
details of nature.'

So where his contemporary John Keats goes off into flights
of fancy in his famous 'Ode to a Nightingale', Clare's own sonnet
about the bird, 'The Nightingale's Nest', is a model of careful
observation and restraint:

I hear the Nightingale,
That from the little blackthorn spinney steals
To the old hazel hedge that skirts the vale
And still unseen, sings sweet – the ploughman feels
The thrilling music as he goes along,
And imitates and listens – while the fields
Lose all their paths in dusk to lead him wrong
Still sings the Nightingale her sweet melodious song.

But by the start of the nineteenth century, this young writer's
whole world – the countryside and its birds – was about to
change forever. The reason for this change was the social and
political movement known as 'enclosure'. Enclosure transformed
the old, traditional landscape of wide, open fields by adding
hedges, creating the familiar pattern of small fields that we know

and love today. Jeremy Burchardt sums up its impact: 'Enclosure was, in crude terms, the privatisation of what had been an open and public landscape.'

Yet as he points out, our love of what we today regard as Britain's classic lowland landscape is based on a misapprehension: 'The irony is that it is a much more recent landscape than we perhaps tend to realise. It only dates back about two hundred or two hundred and fifty years, because before enclosure we didn't have this chequerboard pattern, we had a much more open landscape, with far fewer hedges.'

Enclosure had a devastating effect on ordinary rural people, forcing them off the land and into poverty. For John Clare, the loss of familiar landmarks from his childhood home was a very personal tragedy, and one that eventually tipped him over the edge into clinical depression. In one of his best-known poems, 'The Flitting', written to mourn the effects of enclosure, he summed up the dramatic changes he had witnessed in the simple but memorable phrase: 'all is strange and new'.

But enclosure also had more long-term consequences. By concentrating ownership in the hands of a few rich landowners – who as a result had an economic incentive to maximise production from their land – it would eventually pave the way towards modern, industrial-scale farming. During the following 150 years or so, this would prove disastrous for the British countryside and its birds.

Today, we read Clare's poetry partly as a lament for a lost world; but also because it has a very modern, environmentally conscious message, as Jeremy Mynott notes: 'Now, he begins to look more like a prophet of the kinds of environmental movements that call themselves "deep ecology". He seems to anticipate ideas that are caught up in the Gaia hypothesis, which thinks of the whole world as one organism, with its own interests, and its own self-regulating procedures.'

For a warning of our disconnection from the environment, we need look no further than the plight of one of Clare's most familiar birds, the Corncrake. Even in the decades after Clare's death in 1864, the Corncrake still bred in every county in Britain and Ireland, as well as on most of our larger offshore islands, making it one of the most widespread of all British birds at the time.

But the seeds of the Corncrake's decline had been sown during the early nineteenth century, with the beginnings of the agricultural revolution. In order to feed the growing number of people living in Britain's towns and cities, farmers turned to fertilisers to increase their crop yields. First, they used seabird guano imported from South America; later, as chemical fertilisers became widely available, farmers turned to these to maximise production per acre. This enabled the hay crop to be cut much earlier in the summer, resulting in the destruction of the Corncrake's nests and eggs, or the killing of its tiny chicks.

By the Second World War the Corncrake had vanished from many of its former haunts, and when fieldwork for the first British Trust for Ornithology Atlas survey was carried out, in the late 1960s, the species had disappeared from most of lowland England and Wales. Twenty years later, the second Atlas survey showed that it was more or less confined to the Scottish offshore islands and rural parts of Ireland, where farming practices had not changed.

Since then, thanks to conservation measures carried out by the RSPB to encourage traditional farming, the Corncrake has made a comeback from the low point of the late 1980s. Since then, the number of calling males has more than doubled, from about 600 to about 1,300; and, in a pioneering reintroduction scheme, Corncrakes are also being released on the Nene Washes near Peterborough. Ironically, this is but a short distance, as a bird flies, from Clare's Northamptonshire home.

But given that only a little over a century ago the Corncrake was probably as widespread as the Skylark is today, we can only lament the fate of this mysterious bird, and wonder if it will ever manage to return to anything approaching its former ubiquity.

* * *

Not all countryside birds suffered the fate of the Corncrake. By the middle of the nineteenth century, the fortunes of two other species were on the rise. Together, they would change the face of the British rural landscape forever.

With a collective weight of more than three million tonnes, the Pheasant is, pound for pound, the commonest bird in the countryside. It is, however, not really a British bird at all, but was brought here from south-west Asia by the Romans. The native Red Grouse, by contrast, is a shy, retiring bird, found only in the remotest parts of upland Britain.

But the Red Grouse and the Pheasant do have one thing in common – they are both very good to eat. From the early nineteenth century, thanks to the invention of the breech-loading shotgun, Red Grouse, Pheasants, and their smaller relative the Grey Partridge, became the top targets for Britain's gun-toting sportsmen. This created its own social calendar, providing entertainment from late summer through to the following spring, as

Mark Cocker explains: 'Increasingly you see the development of country estates and landed properties being used for sports shooting, based on three birds: the Red Grouse, Grey Partridge and the Pheasant. These would provide a six-month cycle of recreational activity, where people would move from one country house to another, pursuing the shooting of gamebirds.'

Jeremy Burchardt elaborates on the social importance of the sport – especially Pheasant shooting: 'Pheasant shooting became immensely popular in the nineteenth century; it became one of those key markers of aristocratic identity, one of those "must-have" things; so if you were a landowner you had to have a decent Pheasant shoot.'

But as Jeremy Burchardt points out, ordinary rural folk took a very dim view of this aristocratic pursuit:

> If you want to pick one bird which brought England closer to revolution than any other, I think it would be the Pheasant. It caused bitter social controversy, partly because I think it had become a symbol of aristocratic identity. Actually shooting Pheasants is quite difficult, and demands quite a level of skill, but that isn't obvious; so it seemed a clear instance of decadence, and of the fundamental idleness of the aristocracy: they didn't have anything better to do with their time other than go out and shoot these birds, which were actually only there because the aristocracy had bred them!

For a portrait of the central place Pheasant shooting had attained in British society, we need look no further than the 1985 film *The Shooting Party*. Starring James Mason as a wealthy country landowner hosting a Pheasant shoot on the eve of the First World War, the film's narrative perfectly captures the social tensions created by this aristocratic pursuit. When Lord Gilbert Hartlip, played by Edward Fox, shoots and fatally wounds a working-class beater, his callous indifference to the man's fate tells us everything we need to know about the attitudes of the day.

Such a popular pastime could only be sustained because Pheasants were reared on an industrial scale, and then released in their thousands to replenish birds shot by the sportsmen. And as Jeremy Burchardt explains, the boom in Pheasant shooting was a direct result of the landscape changes brought about by enclosure, and in turn it helped shape this new landscape:

Once enclosure had effectively privatised the countryside, then landowners were able to a much greater extent to develop the land as they wanted. So they planted little copses that were suitable for Pheasants to roost or be bred in, creating a landscape that was first suitable for, and then specifically developed for, Pheasant breeding, rearing and, of course, shooting.

This new, more wooded landscape didn't just benefit Pheasants; it also provided a safe haven for other woodland wildlife, including birds, butterflies and deer. And even though Pheasant shooting has declined since its Victorian and Edwardian heyday, its effects on the British countryside can still be seen today.

* * *

Meanwhile on the windswept moors of northern England and Scotland, another gamebird was also playing its part in changing our landscape, and influencing our history.

The Red Grouse may look like a domestic chicken, but it has had a greater influence on the appearance and economy of upland Britain than any other bird. Although most people will never set eyes on one, its image and reputation have spread far and wide – over the years it has been used to market a wide range of products, including 'The Famous Grouse' Scotch whisky, whose television advertisements memorably feature an animated grouse.

For two groups of people in Britain – aristocrats and the idle rich – the 'Glorious Twelfth' of August has long been the most eagerly awaited date in the calendar. For 12 August marks the opening day of the grouse shooting season; an industry worth at least £30 million a year to the Scottish economy alone. But without the invention of one man, George Stephenson, and the passion of one woman, Queen Victoria, the Red Grouse might have remained nothing more than a shy, and rather unremarkable, moorland bird.

The civil engineer George Stephenson has been called 'The Father of Railways'. His foresight in building the first public steam railway line in the world, the route between Stockton and Darlington that opened in 1825, forever changed the way we travel. It also helped drive the burgeoning Industrial Revolution by allowing the efficient movement of goods and people around the country.

Railways also transformed the fortunes of the grouse shooting industry, as Mark Cocker explains:

> **Previously, the Scottish estates were hundreds of miles and a week's journey from London, but by the 1870s landowners who had posh houses in Chelsea could also own a Scottish country estate, and be there overnight. And that's exactly what happened in the run-up to the Glorious Twelfth of August: there were special trains laid on to channel people to the most remote parts of our landscape, so that this kind of sports shooting could take place on Scottish and northern English moorlands.**

Grouse shooting also received the royal seal of approval, through Queen Victoria's regular visits to her Scottish country estate at Balmoral Castle on Deeside. Victoria and her husband Prince Albert first visited Balmoral in 1848, and loved it so much that they bought the castle and its estate in 1852. Now that the queen had given her seal of approval, the court and its associated hangers-on began to visit the Scottish Highlands too, and indulge in the usual country pursuits of 'hunting, shooting and fishing'.

So, by the end of the queen's long reign, in 1901, grouse

shooting was as much a part of the social calendar as debutantes' coming-out balls and Royal Ascot – though rather more brutal, as Mark Cocker points out: 'In some glorious autumns in the late nineteenth and early twentieth centuries, as many as one and a half million grouse might be shot; today there are fewer than 250,000 pairs of Red Grouse, in total, in the whole of Britain.'

This influx of people and money enabled huge tracts of northern Britain to be opened up for grouse shooting. And because the moors had to be carefully managed to stop them becoming overgrown with scrub and trees, the face of our uplands was changed forever, as Jeremy Burchardt notes:

One of our most cherished landscapes remains heather moorland; and these moors really have been to a very large extent maintained for grouse. The fact that they have been cyclically burned, in order to maintain the young growing shoots of heather for the grouse to feed on, has been really very important in preserving one of Britain's crucial landscape types.

But while grouse and pheasant shooting may have helped to create a new habitat for birds and other wildlife, it sounded the death-knell for Britain's birds of prey, according to Mark Cocker: 'Anything that naturally included Red Grouse or Pheasant or Partridge in its diet became enemy-in-chief, and so the other side of this sophisticated gun technology used to kill grouse was that it was also used to knock off every single bird red in tooth and claw.'

Raptors such as the Buzzard and Sparrowhawk, and opportunistic scavengers such as Rooks, were shot on sight. And even species of bird that posed absolutely no threat to the hunters' quarry were ruthlessly persecuted, as Mark Cocker notes:

> W. H. Hudson, a wonderful writer
> at the beginning of the twentieth century,
> described estates in southern England where
> the gamekeeper would shoot the Nightingale
> because he didn't want the sound of the bird
> disturbing his Pheasants. There are stories of
> gamekeepers shooting any small bird that was
> in the woodland because they would
> be competitors for the grain laid
> out for the gamebirds.

*　　*　　*

Just as the fate of our countryside birds was looking bleak, history intervened; with the coming of the Great War, in August 1914. Ironically, the shooting skills of both the gamekeepers and their masters would prove to be their downfall, for they were among the first to join up and be sent to the front line.

Most of these young men had never been abroad – indeed, some had hardly travelled beyond the borders of their own parish. So any reminders of home, such as the familiar sights and sounds of the British countryside, became powerful totems of the land they had left behind. One of the most potent of these was the song of the Skylark, memorably described by Andrew Motion: 'To pour this amazingly loud, clear, beautiful noise down upon us, sometimes from such a height, and with a body so small, that you can't even see what the source is, that's what makes it like the voice of God.'

The Skylark's extraordinary singing ability is also what appeals to David Attenborough: 'It is this valiant quality that the Skylark has, of suddenly zooming into the air and when it's right up there, singing with such vigour – you'd think it has enough problems remaining up there flapping its wings, but it's got the energy as well to sing!'

Poets and musicians had long appreciated the Skylark's song – in his famous 'Ode to a Skylark', the Romantic poet Percy Bysshe Shelley wrote one of the best-known couplets in English poetry:

Hail to thee, Blithe Spirit!
Bird thou never wert.

But although Shelley goes on to mimic the Skylark's song-flight in his verse, it was the Victorian poet George Meredith who most perfectly captured the rhythms of this extraordinary natural phenomenon, in his poem 'The Lark Ascending':

He rises and begins to round,
He drops the silver chain of sound
Of many links without a break,
In chirrup, whistle, slur and shake,
All intervolved and spreading wide,

Like water-dimples down a tide
Where ripple ripple overcurls
And eddy into eddy whirls...

Meredith's verse inspired Ralph Vaughan Williams to compose his famous musical work of the same name, whose notes and phrases also mimic the rhythms of the Skylark's song.

Yet for much of our history, Britons took a far less romantic, and far more practical, view of this little bird. During Queen Victoria's reign, tens of thousands of Skylarks would be sold for food in places like London's Leadenhall Market. Their importance as a source of protein can be gauged from the contents of popular cookery books of the era. In her bestselling *Mrs Beeton's Book of Household Management*, the eponymous author included a number of recipes using Skylarks, including this one for 'lark pie':

Make a stuffing of bread crumbs, minced lemon-peel, parsley, and the yolk of an egg, all of which should be well mixed together; roll the larks in flour, and stuff them. Line the bottom of a pie-dish with a few slices of beef and bacon; over these place the larks, and season with salt, pepper, minced parsley, and chopped shallot, in the above proportion. Pour in the stock or water, cover with crust, and bake for an hour in a moderate oven. During the time the pie is baking, shake it 2 or 3 times, to assist in thickening the gravy, and serve very hot.

COUNTRYSIDE BIRDS

In the years leading up to the First World War, people's attitude towards Skylarks was an uneasy mixture of the romantic and the utilitarian, with their stomachs often triumphing over their hearts. But the appearance of larks singing in the skies above the fields of conflict in Flanders would change all that forever, and place the Skylark firmly in the pantheon of iconic British birds.

The bird's unique habit of singing so high in the sky, for such long periods of time, meant that the Skylark was often the only bird soldiers hunkered down in their trenches could actually see or hear. Christopher Frayling paints a vivid picture of what it must have been like for them to encounter this familiar bird in such unexpected circumstances: 'Imagine you're in a trench in Flanders, you've been stuck in the ground for three months, you're completely static, you're bogged down; and then this creature appears in the sky with its song. It must have had a huge impact on people – this little creature is everything you want to be.'

One serving soldier, Sergeant Major F. H. Keeling, wrote a poignant letter home, in which he described his mixed feelings about the singing Skylarks: 'Every morning when I was in the front-line trenches I used to hear the larks singing soon after we stood-to about dawn. But those wretched larks made me more sad than anything else out here... Their songs are so closely associated in my mind with peaceful summer days in gardens or pleasant landscapes in Blighty.'

Skylarks also featured in many poems written amidst the horror of war, as Andrew Motion points out:

I suppose the Skylark is the default bird
of First World War poetry, because it rises
above, because it sees things from the air. So
there's that sense of escape, but also of going on
singing when all reasons around you are saying
weep, which is presumably something that would
cheer you if you thought you were going to
get your head blown off at any moment.

The soldier-poet John William ('Will') Streets, a self-educated miner from Sheffield, had joined up at the beginning of the war, enlisting in the 'Sheffield Pals' battalion, part of the York and Lancaster Regiment. While in the trenches he wrote a series of poems, including these memorable lines from 'A Lark Above the Trenches', pointing up the ironic contrast between his own situation and that of the soaring Skylark:

> Hushed is the shriek of hurtling shells: and hark!
> Somewhere within that bit of deep blue sky,
> Grand in his loneliness, his ecstasy,
> His lyric wild and free, carols a lark.
> I in the trench, he lost in heaven afar;
> I dream of love, its ecstasy he sings…

Along with 20,000 of his fellow soldiers, Sergeant Will Streets died on 1 July 1916, the first day of the Battle of the Somme. During a doomed early morning attack on the German trenches he was wounded, but after returning to get first aid he then went out once more to try to rescue a fellow soldier, and was never seen alive again. His body was not recovered for ten months, following which it was buried in the Euston Road Cemetery in Colincamps, close to where he fell. Skylarks still sing there today. After the war, his poems were published in a modest paperback book, entitled *The Undying Splendour*, a posthumous tribute to a brave and sensitive soldier.

*   *   *

During the First World War, Britain's Foreign Secretary was the Liberal politician Edward Grey, who spent eleven years in the post from 1905 to 1916, longer than anyone before or since.

Today, Grey is most famous for the lines he is said to have uttered while gazing out of the windows of the Foreign Office on the eve of the war: 'The lamps are going out all over Europe; we shall not see them lit again in our lifetime.'

In 1916, when he left the Foreign Office, he became Viscount Grey of Fallodon, later serving as the British Ambassador to the United States, and leader of the Liberal Party in the House of Lords.

Edward Grey had a lifelong interest in birds – one he shared with another great world statesman, the twenty-sixth US President, Theodore 'Teddy' Roosevelt. Roosevelt's passion for birds had begun at an early age when, at the age of eight, he began collecting stuffed birds in his native New York City.

He soon saw the light, however, and not long after he became the governor of New York in 1898 he closed down the factories dealing with bird skins and feathers for the fashion trade. In his two terms as President, from 1901 to 1909, he passed a wealth of

bird protection legislation, creating more than fifty wildlife ref-
uges across America.

So when he visited Britain a year after he left office, in the
summer of 1910, it was only natural that he should spend some
time in the company of his fellow enthusiast, Edward Grey. In
June of that year, these two great men went for a quiet country
walk in the New Forest, in Grey's home county of Hampshire.
The scene is described by environmental historian Rob Lambert:
'Putting aside global diplomacy, and talk of military and industrial might and the economy, they simply talked birds. And
President Roosevelt later said that it was the highlight of his
entire European tour in the summer of 1910.'

They saw and heard no fewer than forty different species,
many of which they identified by listening to their song. Grey
was particularly struck by Roosevelt's extraordinary ear for
birds that would have been new and unfamiliar to him, as he
recalled many years later: 'He had one of the most perfectly
trained ears for birdsong I have ever known, so that, if three or
four birds were singing together, he would pick out their songs,
distinguish each, and ask to be told their name...'

What is truly extraordinary, as Rob Lambert points out, is
that despite being two of the leading world statesmen of the era,
they spent the whole day without being followed by a legion of
security men, as would happen nowadays: 'One element of the
story I particularly like is the fact that they did this walk alone.
These two great men, walking through the New Forest, quietly
discussing nature, and wildlife, and the countryside.'

Looking back, Rob Lambert finds it hard to imagine modern
political leaders engaging in such an innocent pastime: 'Margaret

Thatcher and Ronald Reagan had a very strong relationship, but that was based on shared political ideals. The friendship between Roosevelt and Edward Grey was based on a passion – a love for birds – and an appreciation of the British countryside.'

After the war, when he had left high office, Grey returned to his first love: birds. During this period, birdwatching was fast becoming a popular recreational activity, with a flood of bird books aimed not at experts, but at the general public. These included *The Birds of the British Isles and their Eggs*, first published in three volumes in 1920. Written by a cloth-capped Cheshire man, T. A. Coward, this soon became the standard work for bird-watchers wanting to identify the birds they saw. But more refined readers preferred a book written by the aristocratic Edward Grey, entitled *The Charm of Birds*.

Like *The Natural History of Selborne*, *The Charm of Birds* was aimed squarely at a mass audience, as Grey himself makes clear in the preface to the work: 'This book will have no scientific value. Those who have studied birds will not find in it anything that they do not already know; those who do not care for birds will not be interested in the subject... My observations have been made for recreation; in search of pleasure, not knowledge.'

Grey's modesty does him a disservice. *The Charm of Birds* earned its well-deserved popularity and wide readership because he was a perceptive observer, and wrote with an easy, accessible style, perfect for the general reader. His account of Britain's smallest bird, the Goldcrest, is a fine example of personal observation combined with the benefit of a lifetime's experience:

The goldcrest is not an easy bird to
observe, but this is because of its incessant
activity; not because of its shyness. It is not a
shy bird, but this seems due, not so much to
tameness as to indifference: the indifference that
small insects show to large things such as human
beings. Once when I was sitting among whin-
bushes in the New Forest a goldcrest came so
close to my face that it suggested the need of
reading-spectacles to peruse it.

*   *   *

The reference to 'reading-spectacles' reminds us that by the time
Grey was writing *The Charm of Birds*, in the mid-1920s, his eye-
sight was failing fast. So it is hardly surprising that much of his
writing focuses strongly on birdsong. One of his particular
favourites was the Nightingale, although like many listeners his
response to this iconic bird is not without some reservations:
'The nightingale's song has compass, variety and astonishing
power; it arrests attention and compels admiration; it has onset
and impact; but is fitful, broken and restless; it is a song to listen
to, but not to live with.'

This subtle, perceptive and ambivalent response to the
Nightingale's song sums up our long relationship with this mysterious bird. This is despite its rather unprepossessing appearance, as Bill Oddie notes: 'You don't want to see a Nightingale,

actually, because if you do you'll be disappointed! It is just a little brown bird, and maybe that helps with the mystique of them as well – you don't see it, just hear the song.'

And it is the Nightingale's extraordinary song which has been the key to its reputation. It is not the only bird to sing by night, but it is certainly the most persistent. Jeremy Mynott thinks its fame is all the more remarkable, given that it has always been a relatively scarce bird in Britain, confined mainly to woods and heaths in the south and east of the country: 'Everybody thinks they know what a Nightingale is, but very few people have actually heard one, and even fewer have seen one, because the Nightingale is a very mysterious bird. The most extraordinary thing is its volume – it's extraordinarily loud. It's also very rich in its range of notes.'

The Nightingale had of course been celebrated by writers and poets from the Greeks and Romans to Clare and his contemporary John Keats, whose famous 'Ode to a Nightingale' celebrates the constant presence of the bird's song throughout the ages:

Thou wast not born for death, immortal Bird
No hungry generations tread thee down:
The voice I hear this passing night was heard
In ancient days by emperor and clown...

The lasting fame of the Nightingale's song may be because of, rather than despite, the bird's mysterious habits, according to Bill Oddie: 'The idea of something singing at night, a lone voice in the darkness, is going to set your poetic juices running, I would imagine. Is it lonely? Is it singing to its love that will not reply? And there's no other sound, and the sound fills the night.'

During the years between the two world wars, one particular Nightingale achieved unexpected fame. This totally wild bird performed a spontaneous duet with the cellist Beatrice Harrison, in one of the very first live radio outside broadcasts anywhere in the world. Jeremy Mynott, who has investigated the events surrounding this unique musical event, sets the scene: 'The day was 19 May 1924; it was a perfect day for Nightingales. There was a full moon, it was a warm evening, and Beatrice Harrison put on her best frock and played the cello, to an estimated audience of over a million people.'

Beatrice Harrison – and the bird – had created a broadcasting sensation. More than 50,000 listeners wrote to the BBC to praise the programme, and the event was re-staged every year – though presumably with a series of different Nightingales, as they are not a particularly long-lived bird.

The story of the final broadcast, during the Second World War, is just as enigmatic as the very first one, as Jeremy Mynott reveals:

When the time came, as the Nightingale started up, the BBC engineer who was in charge of the sound equipment heard the sound of approaching aircraft, and very wisely he stopped the broadcast because he thought there might be a security risk. But he kept recording it, so we do have the recording, and what you hear is this fleet of British bombers heading for Germany getting closer and closer. And as the crescendo

of noise builds up from the bombers, so
the crescendo of noise builds up from the
Nightingale – and it's the most dramatic
combination of sounds.

*   *   *

Once war with Germany had been declared in September 1939, life for millions of Britons changed overnight. Families were separated as men went off to fight, and children were evacuated to the countryside.

And just as during the First World War, Britain's birds would provide comfort, support and hope at this time of national crisis. Popular songs such as 'A Nightingale Sang in Berkeley Square', written by Eric Maschwitz, and Vera Lynn's famous '(There'll be Bluebirds Over) The White Cliffs of Dover', helped to keep up morale at this difficult time. Meanwhile one young man, James Fisher, did more than anyone else to promote the importance of watching birds as part of what it meant to be British.

Fisher was the David Attenborough of his day: a scientist, writer and broadcaster who frequently appeared on radio and television. Educated at Eton and Oxford, he was an unlikely man of the people. Yet his life's mission was to convert as many of his fellow Britons as possible to the pleasures of birdwatching. Fisher's approach was summed up by the American bird artist and pioneer of popular field guides, Roger Tory Peterson, after the death of his great friend in 1970: 'Versatile and prolific, his writing had a profound influence on popular ornithology, and he bridged the gap between the academic and the layman more effectively than any of his contemporaries.'

As a young man Tony Soper worked with James Fisher at the BBC, and got to know him well: 'James was a superior person in every real sense; he was highly educated, very sociable, good-looking, and he ticked all the right boxes.'

Zoologist, author and broadcaster Desmond Morris was also a good friend of Fisher: 'James was erudite, he was encyclopaedic in his knowledge of birds – in fact he wrote bird encyclopaedias! He could tell you every postage stamp that had a bird on it in the world, for example, and he left a huge legacy of books.'

The most successful of Fisher's many bird books was also one of his simplest. Published in 1941, during the darkest days of the Second World War, *Watching Birds* was a Pelican paperback, priced at just six old pence. This slim volume would go on to sell more than three million copies, and inspire several generations of budding birdwatchers, including Jeremy Mynott:

It was the first serious bird book I read,
and I found it a wonderful book; I think mainly
because it was so inclusive. Here was this eminent
scientist, writing for people like me, telling me this
was a legitimate interest, and that the sort
of records and observations I might make
were worth making, and were part
of some larger picture.

The book is essentially a step-by-step guide for the amateur ornithologist, full of practical hints and tips on how to study birds and how to make an effective contribution to expanding this realm of human knowledge.

But for Fisher, *Watching Birds* had an even more important purpose, as he made clear in the book's preface:

> Some people might consider an apology necessary for the appearance of a book about birds at a time when Britain is fighting for its own and many other lives. I make no such apology… Birds are part of the heritage we are fighting for. After this war ordinary people are going to have a better time than they have had; they are going to get about more… many will get the opportunity, hitherto sought in vain, of watching wild creatures and making discoveries about them. It is for these men and women, and not for the privileged few to whom ornithology has been an indulgence, that I have written this little book.

Stirring stuff – and Fisher was far from alone in his views. A survey carried out in the very same year confirmed people's passion for their rural heritage, as Christopher Frayling points out: 'The vast majority said England is a village green, an old inn sign, the birds of the countryside, the watermill, the winding lane – that's the image of England, at a time when urban England is being flattened.'

Historian of science Helen Macdonald believes that during the crisis of wartime, when the entire focus of the nation was on fighting the common enemy of Fascism, an interest in birds was one of the key ways in which we as a nation defined what it meant to be British: 'Observing birds and watching them became this really strong way of tying the observer and the nation together; by watching birds you become a trustworthy member of your own culture. Birds stood for a kind of rural British identity that was really under threat in this wartime arena.'

James Fisher died in a car accident in September 1970, at the age of just 58. By the time of his death he had seen birdwatching in Britain grow from an elite, minority interest into a national pastime – in no small part because of his own efforts to popularise his lifelong passion for birds.

*   *   *

Meanwhile, back in the dark days of the Second World War, this new enthusiasm for watching birds took hold in some unlikely places. It even became a popular activity among British prisoners of war incarcerated in Germany, despite the obvious limitations, as Helen Macdonald explains: 'The main problem with being in a prisoner-of-war camp was boredom – they had hours, days, weeks, months, to fill, and nothing to do. It was described by one prisoner as being like an endless Sunday afternoon with no prospect of Monday.'

To combat boredom, the prisoners devised all sorts of entertainments, from football tournaments to music hall shows – and, of course, nature study. As Helen Macdonald points out, they did take a little while, however, to fix on the ideal subject: 'There are some wonderful letters where they talk about how they chose the organism they were going to study. At one point they tried to study snails, but apparently that was too boring, even for prisoners of war!'

Birds were, of course, the obvious choice – being both ubiquitous and abundant. One prisoner, John Buxton, decided to study one of the most beautiful of all birds in his prison camp in the Bavarian hills: the Redstart. Closely related to the Robin, this is a fairly common bird in woodland Europe, though in Britain it is mainly confined to the western oakwoods.

John Buxton was an educated and sensitive man, who later became Professor of Poetry at Oxford, and was described in his obituary as 'strongly built, darkly handsome, broad-browed and intelligent'. He had been captured in the early years of the war, during the Norwegian campaign of 1940, and was eventually sent to a prison camp in Bavaria in southern Germany. This turned out to be a blessing in disguise, as the camp was in a river valley surrounded by woodland, ideal for birds.

Along with his fellow POWs – who included a future Director of the RSPB, Peter Conder, and the man who began Operation Osprey, George Waterston – Buxton began taking notes on the different species they saw in and around the camp. In a rare example of wartime cooperation, he even persuaded the distinguished German ornithologist Erwin Stresemann to send him some metal rings and bird books, so that he could study the birds in more depth.

But as his studies continued, he soon became aware of the paradox of captured men studying wild creatures, as Helen

Macdonald points out: 'Of course the thing about these birds that they watched was that they could just leave the camp at any time; and Buxton, who wrote an extraordinary monograph on the Redstart, using his prison camp notes, made a lot of this...'

In the opening chapter of *The Redstart*, published in 1950, John Buxton writes an impassioned description of his thoughts and emotions when studying the birds:

> My redstarts? But one of the chief joys
> of watching them in prison was that they
> inhabited another world than I; and why should
> I call them mine? They lived wholly and
> enviably to themselves, unconcerned in our
> fatuous politics, without the limitations imposed
> all about us by our knowledge. They lived only
> in the moment, without foresight and
> with memory only of things of immediate
> practical concern to them...

But, of course, the birds had another aspect to their lives, as Helen Macdonald points out: 'He also talked about how they didn't just represent freedom, but they also had these invisible barriers that they couldn't cross, they had their territory, so he identified with them in that way as well.'

The 'prison camp ornithologists', as they have been described, didn't simply *watch* birds; they studied them more closely than anyone had, ever before. Their notebooks show page after page of observations, which document in great detail what each bird is doing every minute of the day. Helen Macdonald sees this as a classic case of how the prisoners' day-to-day concerns were transferred to the way they watched and studied the birds: 'What they show is a kind of massive translation of the kinds of things that go on in a prison camp put onto the birds. So here you have men who are obsessively watched all day and all night by guards; and they're watching birds all day and all night.'

Christopher Frayling agrees, and points to the ways in which such close attention to detail would have helped give these captive men a useful tool to survive their period of incarceration:

I think birdwatching in prison camps is obviously partly about freedom – here is a creature that can hop over the wire – but I think also there's a slightly obsessional quality. It passes the time; it helps you to focus on something and to do it well – it's the classic retreat into collecting mania, retreat into classification. You're in this situation which you absolutely can't control, and here's something you can control.

After five long years in captivity, John Buxton was finally released in 1945. He returned to Britain, where he remained active in both academia and ornithology until his death in 1989, a few days before his seventy-seventh birthday.

*　　*　　*

Back on the Home Front, the cinema was one way of escaping the horrors of war, if only for an hour or two. And in one long-forgotten wartime film, *Tawny Pipit*, the arrival of a pair of rare birds in a sleepy English village symbolised the defence of the British countryside. Helen Macdonald is, with a few minor reservations, a fan of the film:

Tawny Pipit is a wonderfully eccentric British piece of film-making. It tells the story of a little village in England that discovers that a pair of Tawny Pipits is nesting in a field just outside the village. There are many characters that are very familiar from this kind of film – there's the eccentric, bumbling colonel, there's the recovering airman who's charged with protecting the birds. And it's really an allegory about looking after refugees, protecting them, involving them in village life, and basically protecting the status quo.

The film's hero and heroine are the young airman Jimmy Bancroft and his girlfriend Hazel Broome, played by Niall MacGinnis and Rosamund John. On a walking holiday in the Cotswolds they stumble across the nesting pipits, and then mobilise the village (a fictional version of Lower Slaughter in the Cotswolds, renamed

'Lipsbury Lea') to help protect them. During the course of the film they fight off the army's tanks, the Ministry of Agriculture, and a dastardly egg-collector, all of which inadvertently or deliberately threaten to destroy the nest.

Tawny Pipit is very much a story of British values, and of a group of disparate people co-operating with each other in defence of these values against a common enemy. Christopher Frayling sees this as the real message of what might on the surface appear to be a rather lightweight story:

> It's very touching, actually; and not just because of the birds, but because of the rural socialism of the idea, that all these people – the elderly colonel, the young corporal who's an ornithologist, the army, the nurse, the recuperating RAF man – they're all in this together, to support these two creatures being able to breed in a British field.

Tawny Pipit may not seem like a very revolutionary film; yet Christopher Frayling believes that its deeper message closely reflects the social and political climate of the time. In his view, for a brief period in the middle of the Second World War Britain came close to becoming what he describes as a 'socialist republic'. Nevertheless, he can also see that the film has another, less serious side: 'It is a bit quaint now, a bit "Ealing comedy" – there is a corner of a foreign field that is forever Ambridge.'

The film's plot necessarily relies on the fact that the Tawny Pipit is a very rare visitor to Britain – indeed, both Julian Huxley and James Fisher had been consulted by the film-makers, and had suggested they choose this particular species. At the time, and indeed nowadays, the Tawny Pipit was a bird of continental Europe, with a range extending from Spain in the southwest to Sweden in the northeast.

But, of course, all these areas were out of bounds because of the hostilities. This presented the man commissioned to film the birds, Eric Hosking, with a major challenge, as Helen Macdonald explains:

It was filmed by the wonderful bird-photographer Eric Hosking, who had serious problems, of course, because there aren't any Tawny Pipits in Britain. So what he had to do was to film similar birds and pretend they were Tawny Pipits – so he filmed Meadow Pipits, but from behind, because from in front they'd show their very characteristic streaked breast. So he really tore his hair out over this movie, and it's quite fun watching it as a birdwatcher because you raise one eyebrow and think to yourself, 'That's not a Tawny Pipit, that's a Meadow Pipit!'

Like all great British propaganda films, everything turns out fine in the end. The chicks hatch, fledge and leave the nest, and the injured airman returns to flying again. All is right with the world.

Even by the standards of the day, there's no doubt that *Tawny Pipit* portrays an idealised vision of the English countryside, unchanging, and steeped in old-fashioned values. But in reality, things in rural Britain during wartime were very different indeed.

*   *   *

A Pathé newsreel from the middle of the war reveals an extraordinary difference in attitudes towards wild places from that we would hold today. Entitled *Food from Waste Land*, it celebrates the conversion of what is described in the commentary as 'the 6,000-acre wilderness of Feltwell Fen... where nothing grew save weeds and reeds' into productive agricultural land.

On first viewing, this appears to be an overt piece of propaganda from the Ministry of Food, in which the destruction of our precious countryside is not only encouraged, but celebrated. But if we consider the dire situation at the time, it becomes clear that we cannot judge the film by the same standards as today. Ever since the start of the Second World War there had been national food shortages, exacerbated by the fact that much of Britain's food had traditionally been imported from our colonies in Africa and Asia. With the German navy setting up sea blockades all around our coasts, much of this food was simply not getting through.

As the hostilities dragged on, with severe rationing of food and the prospect of widespread starvation, desperate measures had to be taken. So, as the Pathé film shows, huge swathes of our countryside were ploughed up for agriculture. This may have solved the problem of food shortages, but unfortunately at the same time it destroyed some of our most valuable wildlife habitats forever, as Mark Cocker explains:

The entire emphasis was on maximising production, and you can only do that by taking out what you call the 'waste land'. And waste land included half of all our ancient woodlands, 70 per cent of our heathlands, I think we've now lost 99 per cent of our flower-rich meadows – any habitat that wasn't yielding agricultural produce was converted to arable or farming in some way.

Rob Lambert believes that the changes in the countryside, and the way they were simply accepted by the general public, showed a touching faith in the government's planning abilities. Rigorous planning – a process that until then had worked reasonably well in our towns and cities – was not quite so successful when applied to the countryside: 'The irony was that the more we planned, and organised, and structured the future of the British countryside, the more we lost sight of some of these aesthetic and romantic impulses that people had for the countryside and for the birds that lived within it.'

Even after the conflict ended in 1945, food shortages continued, with rationing going on well into the 1950s – longer than the six years of the war itself. During this post-war era, the juggernaut of the modern agricultural revolution was unstoppable, fuelled by the growth of subsidies and new technology.

It was goodbye to the old-fashioned values of *Tawny Pipit*, and welcome to the brave new world of men in white coats. And as Rob Lambert points out, the boffins working in their laboratories came up with what appeared to be the perfect solution to improving productivity:

There was a bright new future for Britain, not only for our industry, but also for the countryside. And so in the late 1950s, and into the 1960s, we sought to get rid of inefficient farming methods and systems, and replace them with cutting-edge new technologies of the time. And one of those technologies was the application of pesticides, and the birth of what we now know as 'chemical farming'.

Chris Baines explains the sense of wonder and relief these new technologies must have evoked at the time: 'You suddenly had this interesting combination of a bunch of chemicals that could kill pests, and a need to increase food production. And at face value it must have seemed very straightforward – you get more of a crop if you remove the weeds, because the crop gets all the food from the soil.'

Productive they may have been, but these revolutionary new farming methods were having devastating effects on the populations of our countryside birds. As well as the widespread use of

pesticides, another major problem was the destruction of traditional habitats, as Chris Baines explains:

> It was degrading the whole landscape, and a lot
> of the wildlife depended on the wild plants, the
> rough edges, the wet bits, and so on and so forth.
> And if you spent lots of time and effort wiping
> out the so-called 'pests', what that meant was
> you killed the moths, the butterflies, the
> caterpillars – and you actually removed
> that element of the food chain.

As a result of the indiscriminate use of chemical pesticides and
herbicides, and the ploughing up of ancient meadows, the populations of many farmland birds went into freefall. Eventually,
environmentalists woke up to what was happening, and began to
warn against the catastrophe of what American environmentalist
Rachel Carson famously called a 'Silent Spring', in her book of
the same name. Published in 1962, *Silent Spring* soon became a
bestseller on both sides of the Atlantic, provoking a debate, and
a series of campaigns, which would eventually turn the tide
against the indiscriminate use of pesticides in North America
and Britain.

But when it came to a choice between farming and birds,
there could only be one winner, as Jeremy Burchardt notes:

There was a kind of illusion, in government and actually in society more widely, that what was good for agriculture was good for the countryside. People believed that the countryside was safe in the hands of farmers. But I think that no one had actually grasped the fact that there was a difficult choice to be made, between maximising agricultural production and attempting to maintain a rich, diverse wildlife in the countryside.

One man who witnessed the calamity in the countryside at first hand was the author Henry Williamson, whose books, including *Tarka the Otter*, had made him a household name. In the BBC film *The Vanishing Hedgerows*, made in 1973, four years before he died, the septuagenarian writer recalled his own experience of agricultural pesticides: 'After the [Second World] war, when I had sold my farm and returned to north Devon and my writing, the general use of other sprays on arable and other grasslands caused the deaths of a great number of birds, including such predators as Sparrowhawks, owls and Buzzards.'

In one of the film's most moving moments, Williamson recalled finding a family of Grey Partridges in one of his fields, all poisoned by chemicals: 'I came across the two birds, crouched side by side in death, with their chicks slightly larger than bumblebees, cold between the protecting feathers.'

Even the largest and most powerful birds – Britain's birds of prey – were not immune to the effects of what turned out to be a chemical time-bomb. Ironically, this new blow to their fortunes occurred just at the point at which their populations were beginning to recover from decades of persecution, as Rob Lambert explains:

Birds of prey that struggled through the nineteenth century, surviving the persecution by gamekeepers to protect landowning interests, had bounced back a little during both the world wars, when many of the gamekeepers were posted overseas. But they were hit tremendously hard by the chemical farming revolution of the 1950s and 1960s. The poison that had been put onto the crops was concentrated up the food chain in the bodies of smaller birds, which were taken as prey items by birds of prey, and they were producing infertile eggs, or indeed eggshells that were so thin they cracked under the incubating birds.

The populations of Buzzards, Peregrines and Sparrowhawks plummeted, although our commonest species, the Kestrel, did manage to escape the worst effects of the chemical revolution. But as Chris Baines remembers, it did so, ironically, by taking advantage of a new habitat created by us:

We went through a period when the
only place you saw Kestrels was along the
motorway verges, because they were long
corridors that were excused agricultural
improvement. Nobody was spraying the road
verges, so you hadn't got that kind of damage;
and the birds of prey that survived were those
that learned to feed over the verges, and you
didn't see them over the fields. But for some
species, it was almost the end.

The pesticide DDT – the main culprit amongst these agricultural chemicals – was finally banned in Britain in 1984, more
than forty years after the destruction of our countryside and its
birds had begun.

*   *   *

Since then, different groups of birds have experienced very different fortunes. Birds of prey have been the fastest to make a
comeback, not only because of the banning of DDT, but also
because in many parts of the country they are no longer persecuted as ruthlessly as they were in the past. Golden Eagles,
Buzzards and Red Kites are now a far more regular sight in our
skies. Adaptable groups of birds such as crows and pigeons have
also fared well, as they are able to take advantage of a variety of
man-made habitats to find food and places to nest.

But the fate of many of our smaller rural birds could hardly be more different. The continuing drive to make agriculture more productive has been a disaster for birds that depend on farmland. Hedgerows have continued to be destroyed, hay meadows plighted up, and although DDT is no longer available, chemical insecticides and herbicides are still widely used today, in order to increase crop yields. As a result, many species of farmland bird continue to decline, and have vanished from their former haunts.

That favourite bird of the poets, the Skylark, has suffered particularly badly. Changes in the patterns of the planting of arable crops, especially the widespread sowing of winter wheat, have dramatically reduced the amount of available food for the Skylark, while the spread of monocultures such as wheat and barley has reduced their breeding habitat too.

In the first BTO Atlas survey, from 1968 to 1972, the Skylark was our most widespread bird, found in about 98 per cent of all 10-kilometre squares. Today it is still found across much of Britain, but numbers have fallen dramatically, with declines of about 60 per cent from the late 1970s to the present day – the loss of well over one million breeding pairs in the space of a single human generation.

And the Skylark is not the only bird of the farmed countryside to have suffered such a dramatic decline. Birds such as the Corn Bunting, Turtle Dove, Linnet and Yellowhammer have all seen their numbers drop by between 50 and 80 per cent. Overall, since 1970, our farmland bird populations have fallen by about half.

So these dramatic changes have happened not gradually, over centuries, but suddenly, during our own brief lifetimes, as Bill Oddie recalls:

I can remember, as a teenager in the
1950s, walking across what I wouldn't regard
as anything except normal farmland, and
Lapwings coming up, Skylarks coming up that
were nesting there. In winter there would be
a flock of maybe a hundred or two hundred
Yellowhammers, and other finches and buntings
among them – in other words, more birds
than today, absolutely no question about
that whatsoever.

Brought up in rural Essex a decade or so later, Andrew Motion
has similar memories from the 1960s:

I can remember riding around the
headlands of fields in the autumn, and clouds
of Lapwings pretty much blackening the sky,
rising up out of the newly ploughed ground,
and masses and masses of Skylarks, and masses
and masses of finches – and that was only forty-
five years ago. And when I see a Lapwing now,
I take my hat off to it – it feels like a rarity.

Although they are waders – members of the plover family – Lapwings spend much of their lives on farmland. They spend the autumn and winter in large flocks on open fields, and in spring and summer make their nests on rough grassland. In the fifty years since 1960, more or less the span of Mark Cocker's lifetime, their numbers have fallen by four-fifths: 'For me, the fate of the Lapwing is a kind of personal tragedy – it's almost autobiographical. They are beautiful, they sound fantastic, they remind me of my childhood; they remind me of the landscape, and they are somehow synonymous with a diverse landscape.'

The loss of these familiar birds is a timely warning about the current state of the British countryside, and the damage we have done. But its significance goes far deeper than that. We are now beginning to realise that their fate, and the fate of all our wildlife, is inextricably linked with our own emotional and spiritual well-being. According to David Attenborough: 'Human beings have suddenly, in my lifetime, begun to understand that the presence of a healthy community of mammals and birds and reptiles and insects is absolutely of huge importance to the health of the human spirit.'

Jeremy Mynott, who began watching birds in the 1950s, inspired by James Fisher's little paperback book on the subject, warns us how easy it is to overlook the disappearance of our countryside birds: 'The loss of these birds matters because it is, in the end, an impoverishment. It happens quite gradually, so you don't notice it – like you don't notice your hair going grey – but it happens, and when it's happened, you then notice it.' And if these birds were to vanish altogether, he believes our very concept of 'countryside' would be under threat: 'If birds disappeared from the countryside, it wouldn't mean the same to call it the "countryside" – it would be the "non-urban spaces".'

Andrew Motion takes a similar view: 'If birds went out of the countryside – "The sedge is withered from the lake, and no birds sing," to quote Keats, it would be an emblem of a kind of post-nuclear deadness. To live in a silent world would be a really dreadful thing.'

EPILOGUE

The story of our nation's relationship with birds has been a long, eventful, and often stormy one. So how is this relationship likely to develop in the future? Will it fade and decline, as our lives become ever more remote from nature? Or will it grow and strengthen, as we realise that we need birds – and the connection they give us to the natural world – at least as much as birds need us?

*   *   *

The main way in which the vast majority of Britons continue to encounter birds is likely to be, as it was for much of the latter half of the twentieth century, from their back window. Our passion for garden birds looks unlikely to abate: a survey by the RSPB revealed that two out of three households regularly put out food to attract birds.

The importance of this national obsession was revealed in the successive hard winters of 2009-10 and 2010-11, when snow and ice in the wider countryside drove huge numbers of birds into our gardens. This had two main consequences: first, it meant that many people began to notice species they had not seen before, such as the Fieldfare and Redwing. But it also had a profound effect on the fate of the birds themselves, with smaller species such as the Long-tailed Tit surviving in far greater numbers than they would have in previous hard winters, when far fewer people provided food for birds. Assuming we continue to feed garden birds through future snowy winters, this may eventually have a positive effect on the populations of some of our most vulnerable birds.

The fact that it helps our fellow creatures is clearly one reason why feeding garden birds – and providing places for them to drink, bathe and nest – is so popular. But there are less altruistic reasons why we do it, too. Attracting birds to our gardens is a form of home entertainment, no less central to many people's lives than the alternative attractions of television and the Internet. Indeed garden birds have been given their very own TV show in the form of the highly popular *Springwatch*, whose loyal audience follows the fortunes of its lead characters with all the passion that other people devote to watching more conventional soap operas.

Technology will continue to drive this aspect of our obsession with birds: through developments in high-energy foods to suit particular species, and also through the growing popularity of cameras in nestboxes, specially designed and marketed to allow people to recreate the *Springwatch* experience in their own back gardens, with 'their' birds.

Garden birds have another vital role to play. For many people they are the gateway to a wider interest in birds, beyond the boundaries of their own home. Many children learn about birds primarily in this domestic setting, especially now that for many of them the wider countryside is more or less out of bounds. Later in life, perhaps, their early encounters with Robins and Goldfinches may spark a deeper curiosity about birds.

*   *   *

Meanwhile, our waterbirds, and the places where they live, are undergoing what can justly be described as a revolutionary change. Bird protection began during the late nineteenth century with the impulse to save waterbirds such as grebes and egrets from being sacrificed to the whims of fashion. This soon developed into bird conservation, which was mainly carried out by fencing off small and discrete patches of land as nature reserves.

During much of the twentieth century this worked fairly well: it safeguarded the birds, retained areas of habitat for them to breed or spend the winter, and allowed people to come and see them. Waterbirds remained at the forefront of our conservation strategy, partly because they are so visible and spectacular, but also because many of the RSPB reserves, and all of the WWT centres, are wetlands – Minsmere, Titchwell and Slimbridge, to name but three.

But towards the end of the last century, as the problems of habitat loss began to increase, and the effects of climate change started to be felt, we realised that the strategy of creating and preserving 'islands' in the form of nature reserves was not necessarily the best way to combat these new threats. What was needed was an entirely new and far more ambitious approach:

EPILOGUE

the large-scale 'rewilding' of huge areas of the countryside – in effect the creation, from scratch, of entirely new habitats.

Wetlands are at the forefront of this approach, for one very good reason. They are by far the easiest habitat to make: former quarries, peat diggings, gravel-pits or even arable fields can be transformed in just a few years. With careful management techniques, including the planting of extensive reedbeds and the creation of open pools, a new wetland can be created in a very short time – much quicker, for instance, than it would take to create an ancient woodland.

The Somerset Levels, already one of our largest remaining areas of wetland, is the classic example of major landscape change. The area where the Cranes are now being reintroduced has been utterly transformed, attracting a suite of new colonists such as Little, Cattle and Great White Egrets, all of which have taken advantage of climate change to extend their ranges northwards from continental Europe into Britain. Bitterns, too, have continued their comeback following their near-fatal decline as a British breeding bird, and have now spread into this new wetland from farther east. As an example of landscape-scale conservation, the Somerset Levels could hardly be bettered.

But climate change is not such good news for enthusiasts of wintering wildfowl – the millions of ducks, geese and swans which head south and west from their Arctic breeding grounds each autumn to take advantage of our mild winter climate. Despite a couple of harsh winters in Britain recently, the long-term trend towards milder winters has tempted many of these birds to stay closer to their breeding grounds; or to leave our shores in late winter rather than early spring. So numbers of familiar winter visitors such as Bewick's and Whooper Swans and White-fronted Geese are falling off; and should the warming trend continue, these birds may choose to spend the winter across the North Sea in the Netherlands, or even around the Baltic Sea.

*   *   *

Many of the ancient ways in which our ancestors related to the birds around them have now largely disappeared. The hunter-gatherer existence of the 'bird people' of St Kilda may have lasted well into the twentieth century, but this was an historical anomaly – such practices had long since died out around the rest of our coasts.

As we have seen, as our status as a maritime nation declined, so seabirds gradually receded from our consciousness. Only in the late twentieth century did a combination of food shortages on the coast and opportunities to feed and breed inland lead one group of seabirds – gulls – to intrude upon our lives in a new, and not always welcome, way. In the meantime we have become increasingly aware of a decline in fortunes of the 'true' seabirds – species such as Guillemots and Razorbills, Kittiwakes and Puffins, skuas and terns – those which are so suited to an ocean-going lifestyle that they are simply unable to adapt to change in the way that the more opportunistic gulls have managed to do.

Our marine environment has often been ignored in favour of more accessible terrestrial habitats, but in recent years this has begun to change. A realisation that our land-based existence is linked with, and in many ways dependent on, the fortunes of the seas that surround us has gradually taken hold. Seabirds are now playing a vital role in drawing our attention to the problems of global climate change; and we can only hope that despite their continued remoteness from our daily lives, we will be able to save them, and the seas and oceans where they live, before it is too late.

*   *   *

The fate of the birds of our wider countryside is also in the balance, though for other, more complex reasons. Despite many claims to the contrary, from successive governments and lobby groups of vested interests, many of our farmland birds continue to show steep and potentially irreversible declines. Driven by a combination of government policies and consumer demand, farming continues to be mainly about yields and productivity at the expense of our natural heritage, and with an inexorable rise in the global price of food now forecast, this state of affairs seems unlikely to change.

As a result, it is hard not to be pessimistic about the future of iconic birds such as the Skylark, Grey Partridge, Yellowhammer and Lapwing, as their numbers drop to a shadow of their former state, and they disappear from so many places where they were once common and widespread. Our only hope is that the voices raised against their decline are finally heard, and triumph over the vocal minority of those who still see the countryside primarily as a food factory.

Other birds of the countryside are suffering from what is termed a 'double whammy' – problems at home and abroad. Migrants such as the Swallow, House Martin, Nightingale and Cuckoo have also seen population declines in the past few decades, partly due to habitat loss and food shortages here in Britain, but also as a result of problems on their stopover and wintering grounds to and from, and in, Africa. The scientist Peter Berthold once predicted that migrant birds would enjoy a brief 'honeymoon period' as a result of climate change, before they experienced sudden population crashes; if that is the case, the honeymoon does now appear to be well and truly over.

*　　*　　*

Meanwhile, we continue to interact with Britain's birds in a range of very different ways. The 'Glorious Twelfth' of August is still a key date in the sporting calendar, even though those who actually shoot the grouse are more likely to be rich bankers or foreign oligarchs than the landed gentry and aristocracy. The cheaper and more accessible alternative of shooting Pheasants and Partridges also survives in much of lowland England, albeit on a smaller scale than in its Victorian heyday.

Birds have also continued to be an inspiration to artists from all areas of culture, high and low. Modern poets use the behaviour, folklore and imagery of birds as freely as did their Romantic forebears; while birds feature widely in the visual arts, music and literature, as well as in popular culture. The protean nature of birds – their ability to mean different things, to different people, at different times – along with their obvious aesthetic and symbolic qualities, mean that they are likely to continue to inspire artists for the foreseeable future.

As a recreational activity, birding is more popular than ever before; and more popular, indeed, than those of us who have been lifelong birdwatchers could have ever imagined. Every weekend bird reserves up and down the country are thronged with visitors; helped by a huge change in attitudes from those who own and run them.

Not all that long ago, back in the 1970s when I was a young birder, you had to apply in advance, in writing, for a permit to visit the RSPB's flagship reserve at Minsmere; and even then, the reserve was only open on three or four days a week. For many wardens (this was before the days when they were rebranded as 'managers'), members of the public were regarded as an inconvenient by-product of running a reserve, who should be kept as far away from the birds (especially rare breeding species) as possible.

But gradually, thanks in no small part to the pioneering work of men like George Waterston at Loch Garten, these protectionist attitudes began to change, and the conservation bodies realised that their reserves were the ideal way both to keep their existing members happy, and to attract new ones. Today, most reserves boast a café and a shop, enabling some visitors to have a fulfilling day out without ever actually going out to watch the birds. Encounters with birds can also happen in very different settings, with watchpoints at urban and rural locations up and down the country, which allow 'non-birders' to observe rare breeding birds, often for the first time.

One noticeable feature, however, is that the majority of visitors to bird reserves, and indeed birders elsewhere, are from the older generations. This has led to fears that perhaps we are about to see the pastime of birding embark on a long, slow decline, as younger generations fail to take up the baton handed to them by their elders. The phenomenon of 'Nature Deficit Disorder' – the absence, among young people, of engagement with the natural world – is partly to blame for this state of affairs, as youngsters are no longer free to roam the countryside in the way that they were when I was growing up.

Yet a concern for the wider global environment is at least as strong for young people as it is for anyone else. If they can channel their passion for the fate of the Amazon rainforest into places and wildlife closer to home, perhaps we shall see a renaissance in interest in birds among these new generations. And because birds are the most obvious, widespread and beautiful creatures in the natural world, it is likely that a passion for watching them will continue to flourish and spread.

*   *   *

Birds also have two other vital roles to play: roles that may help safeguard our future, as well as theirs. Their ubiquity and mobility means that they respond to environmental change more quickly – and often more visibly – than most creatures. In a rapidly changing world, where habitat loss, overpopulation and climate change are ever-growing threats, birds are already acting as a modern 'miner's Canary': a clear warning against environmental catastrophe. They offer us one last chance: the opportunity to realise that things are going wrong, so we are able to remedy the situation before it is too late.

But birds have a more positive function, too. Like all elements of the natural world, they provide an emotional and spiritual connection between our busy, frantic, day-to-day lives and the

EPILOGUE

wider world in which we all live. They are a gateway through which we can pass, enabling us to put our own lives into perspective; to escape from our everyday problems; to refresh our tired minds; and ultimately to connect with something far greater than ourselves.

Our distant ancestors, watching out for the Swallow returning from its travels to signal the coming of spring, knew this; as did those soldiers crouching in their trenches during the First World War, listening to a distant Skylark pouring out its song in the heavens above.

For many centuries, as our forebears struggled to survive in a hostile and difficult world, they regarded birds purely as objects to be used for their own benefit – at first for food and fuel, and later for sport and recreation. But over time we gradually came to value them, to cherish them, and finally to understand what they truly mean to us. Now birds are waiting to take us on the journey into the future – soaring high into the clear blue sky, and daring us to follow.

FURTHER READING

GENERAL

A Bird in the Bush: a Social History of Birdwatching,
by Stephen Moss (Aurum)

Birders: Tales of a Tribe, by Mark Cocker (Jonathan Cape)

Birds Britannica, by Mark Cocker and Richard Mabey
(Chatto & Windus)

Birdscapes: Birds in our Imagination and Experience,
by Jeremy Mynott (Princeton University Press)

The History of British Birds, by D. W. Yalden and
U. Albarella (Oxford University Press)

Further Reading

*Man and the Natural World: Changing Attitudes in England
1500–1800,* by Keith Thomas (Allen Lane)

The Oxford Book of British Bird Names,
by W. B. Lockwood (Oxford University Press)

The Running Sky, by Tim Dee (Jonathan Cape)

The Shell Bird Book, by James Fisher
(Ebury Press & Michael Joseph)

The Wisdom of Birds, by Tim Birkhead (Bloomsbury)

Garden Birds

The Garden Bird Handbook by Stephen Moss (New Holland)

The History of British Birds, by Revd. F. O. Morris

The Life of the Robin, by David Lack (Witherby)

Redbreast: the Robin in Life and Literature, by Andrew Lack
(SMH Books)

The Secret Lives of Garden Birds by Dominic Couzens (Helm)

The Sparrows, by Denis Summers-Smith (Poyser)

WATERBIRDS

The Eye of the Wind: an Autobiography, by Peter Scott
(Hodder & Stoughton)

A Life of Ospreys, by Roy Dennis (Whittles Publishing)

The Return of the Sea Eagle, by John Love
(Cambridge University Press)

SEABIRDS

The Great Auk, by Errol Fuller (Errol Fuller)

The Guga Hunters, by Donald Murray (Birlinn)

The Herring Gull's World, by Niko Tinbergen (Collins)

The Life and Death of St Kilda, by Tom Steel
(The National Trust for Scotland)

St Kilda Summer, by Kenneth Williamson
and J. Morton Boyd (Hutchinson)

Who Killed the Great Auk?, by Jeremy Gaskell
(Oxford University Press)

FURTHER READING

COUNTRYSIDE BIRDS

The Barley Bird: Notes on the Suffolk Nightingale,
by Richard Mabey (Full Circle Editions)

The Charm of Birds, by Edward Grey
(Weidenfeld and Nicholson)

Crow Country, by Mark Cocker (Jonathan Cape)

The Natural History of Selborne, by Gilbert White
(various editions)

The Poetry of Birds, edited by Simon Armitage
and Tim Dee (Penguin Viking)

The Redstart, by John Buxton (Collins)

Say Goodbye to the Cuckoo, by Mike McCarthy (John Murray)

Watching Birds, by James Fisher (Pelican)

ACKNOWLEDGEMENTS

As with any television series, many people were involved in the production of *Birds Britannia*. The idea came initially from myself and my colleague at the BBC Natural History Unit, Chris Cole, who persuaded the Controller of BBC Four, Richard Klein, of the merit in taking a sideways look at the relationship between birds and the British.

Richard and his team were supportive and encouraging throughout, displaying a benign lack of interference rare in the modern broadcasting world. Our Executive Producer, the aptly-named Neil Nightingale, was also very supportive.

Producer Susie Painter took charge of the *Garden Birds* and *Seabirds* episodes, combining her academic background as an environmental historian with her strong editorial skills to create two compelling episodes. Archive Researcher Carmen Locke was determined to get hold of the very best archive material, at the best possible value; the results of her efforts are clear to see in the depth and quality of the film footage and stills used in the

ACKNOWLEDGEMENTS

series. Production Manager Sophie Cole steered us through the low budget minefield with great skill and experience. All three also read the draft chapters of this book and made many helpful comments and suggestions.

I should also like to thank the other members of the production team: researcher Caitlin Arden, team assistant Deborah Hunt and edit assistant Tom Rowe; the various members of the camera, sound and online teams; and especially the two editors who brought such creativity to their work, Dilesh Korya and Deborah Williams. Bill Paterson narrated the programmes with his unique combination of warmth, humour and authority.

The qualities of a book and archive series such as this owe a great deal to the knowledge, experience and expertise of those interviewed. So I should like to offer very special thanks to: Sir David Attenborough, Professor Chris Baines, Professor Tim Birkhead, Dr Jeremy Burchardt, Mark Cocker, Roy Dennis, Jane Fearnley-Whittingstall, Professor Sir Christopher Frayling, Jeremy Gaskell, Kate Humble, Dr Rob Lambert, David Lindo, Helen Macdonald, Dr William M. Mathew, Dr Frederick Milton, Dr Desmond Morris, Andrew Motion, Donald Murray, Dr Jeremy Mynott, Bill Oddie, Tony Soper, Denis Summers-Smith, Jenny Uglow and Chris Whittles.

The book was commissioned by my old friend Myles Archibald at HarperCollins, with the help of the BBC NHU's Commercial and Business Manager, Ailish Heneberry, and Daniel Mirzoeff from the BBC's Commercial Agency. Julia Koppitz oversaw the project with her usual tact and efficiency, while Yeti McCaldin designed the cover with great skill and care. Helen Brocklehurst did an excellent job in copy-editing and suggesting changes to make the text read more fluently.

BIRDS BRITANNIA

Finally, I should like to thank the two men to whom this book is dedicated: Tony Soper and Bill Oddie. I have had the great privilege of working with them both during my BBC career, and cannot think of anyone else who has done more to promote the British love of birds through the mass media. As their contributions to *Birds Britannia* reveal, they have lost none of the boyish enthusiasm, sense of humour and deep insight which has made them so deservedly popular during their long and distinguished careers in broadcasting.

INDEX

INDEX

Birkhead, Tim 24, 27, 28, 39, 46–7, 60, 72, 77, 87, 88–9, 146, 148, 163, 165

Bittern 68, 69, 75, 77, 80, 116, 117, 231

Blackbird 16, 47, 59, 60, 65

Black-browed Albatross 133

Blackcap 56

Black-headed Gull 146

Black-tailed Godwit 75

Blake, William 23

Bleak House (Dickens) 22–3

Blue Peter 46

Blue Tit 18, 46, 47–8, 59, 60, 61, 65

Braer 163

British Ornithologists' Union 140

British Society for the Advancement of Science 149

British Trust for Ornithology (BTO) 50, 60, 93, 176, 187, 222

Britton, Barrie 28

Brown Pelican 143

Budgerigar 21

Burchardt, Jeremy 19, 142, 144, 179–80, 185, 186, 189, 190, 193, 218–19

Buxton, John 209–11

Buzzard 194, 219, 220, 221

C

caged birds 21–4, 51, 156

Canary 21, 24, 64, 236

Cavendish, Marchioness of Newcastle, Margaret 33

census, bird 93, 164

Chaffinch 47, 57

Chance, Edgar 93

Charm of Birds, The (Grey) 201–2

Chiffchaff 179

Citizen Science 10

CJ Wildbird Foods 55

Clare, John 183–5, 186–7, 188

Clean Air Act, 1956 166

'cleit' 129–30

climate change 169, 230, 231, 233, 234, 236

Club Row, London 21–2

Coal Tit 47

Cocker, Mark 8, 17, 18, 36, 38–9, 40, 42, 48, 49–50, 53, 57, 60, 73, 75–6, 77–8, 80, 85, 86, 110–11, 119–20, 125–6, 127, 129, 130, 131, 135 140, 142, 145, 147, 148, 151, 153–4, 167, 177, 180, 189, 192, 193, 194, 216, 224

Collared Dove 48–50, 53

Collins New Naturalist series 157

Conder, Peter 209

conservation 45, 92, 98–9, 100, 102, 103, 105, 107, 110, 117, 119, 120, 141, 155, 167, 187–8, 230, 231, 235 *see also* protection, bird

cooking for birds 54

Coot 182

Cormorant 155–6

Corn Bunting 117, 178, 222

Corncrake 182, 183, 185, 187–8

countryside birds 171–225
  agriculture and 181–2, 185–7, 216, 217–23
  connection with 9, 172–6
  eating 196, 197
  First World War and 194–9, 205
  future of 233
  hunting/shooting 188–94
  poetry and 182–8, 195–6, 197–8, 203

INDEX

INDEX

INDEX